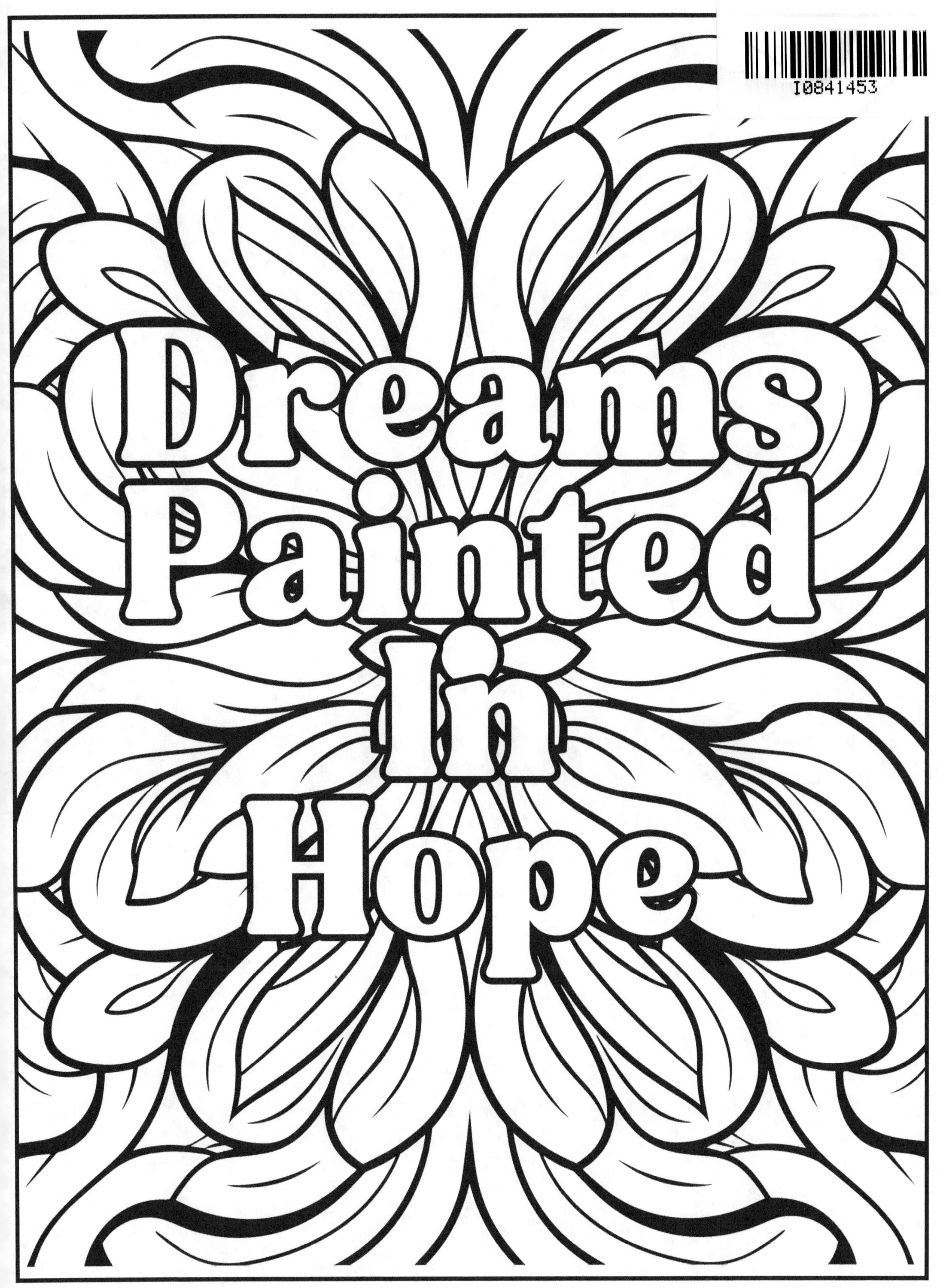
Dreams
Painted
In
Hope

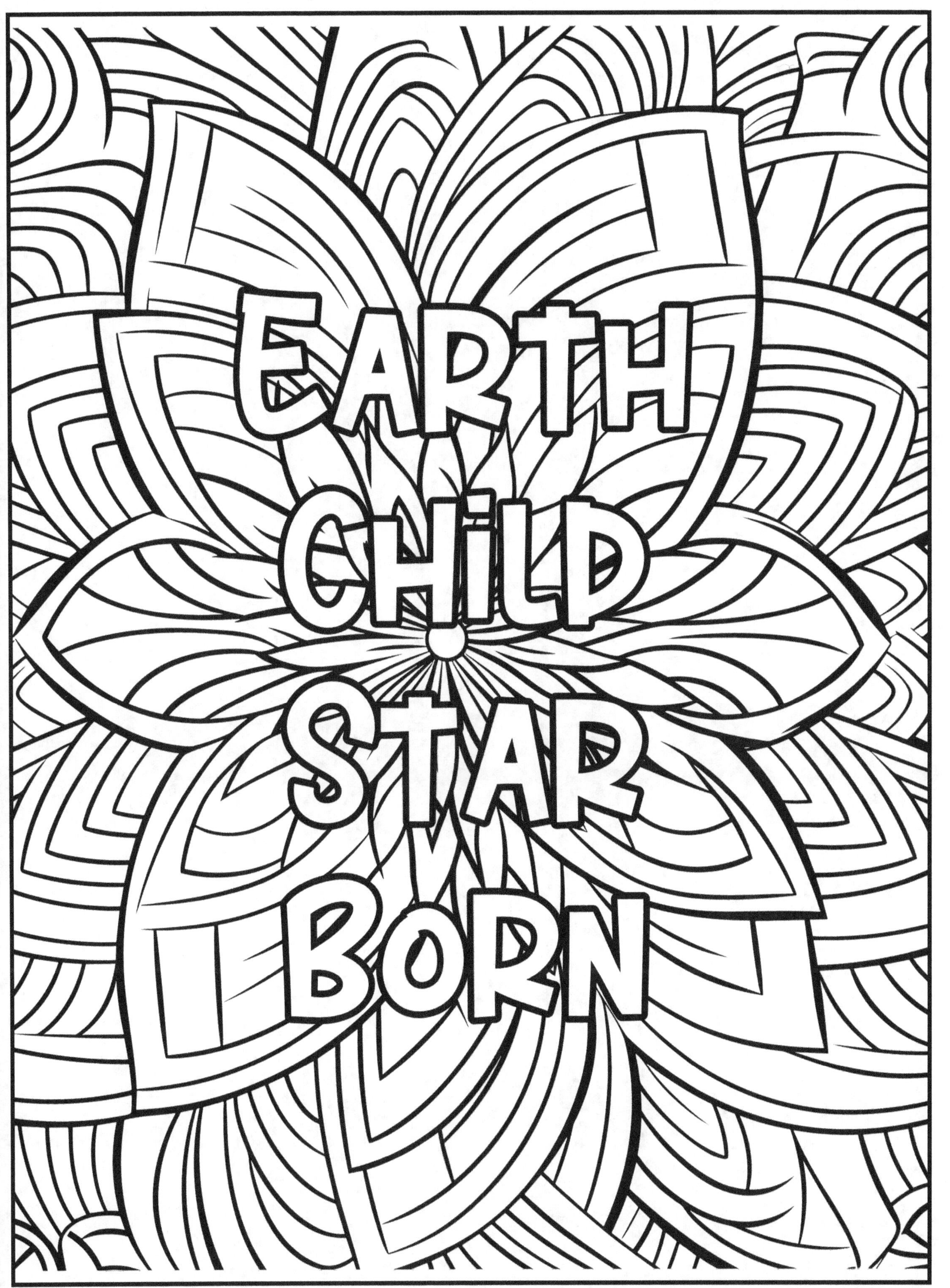

EARTH
CHILD
STAR
BORN

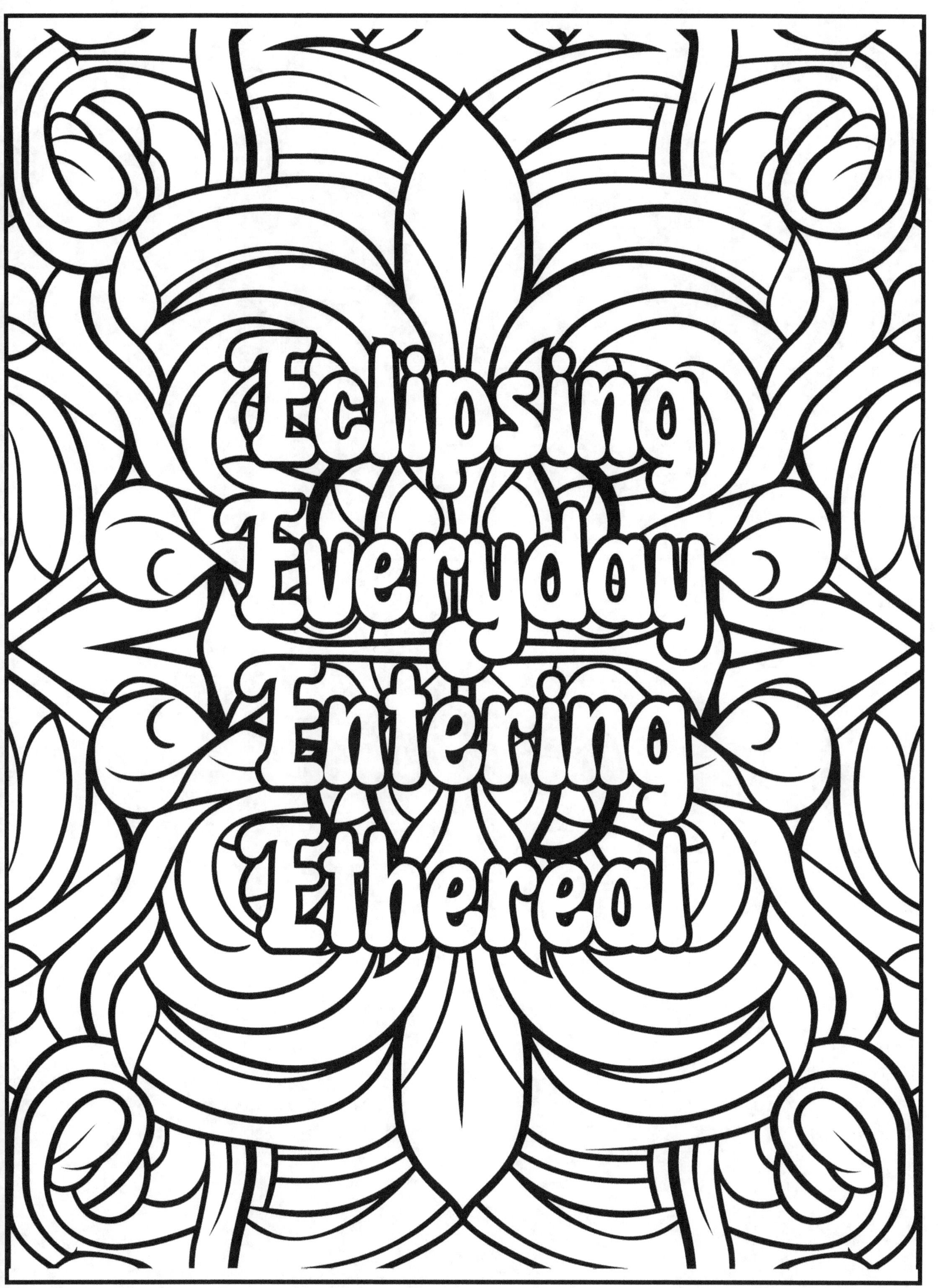

Eclipsing
Everyday
Entering
Ethereal

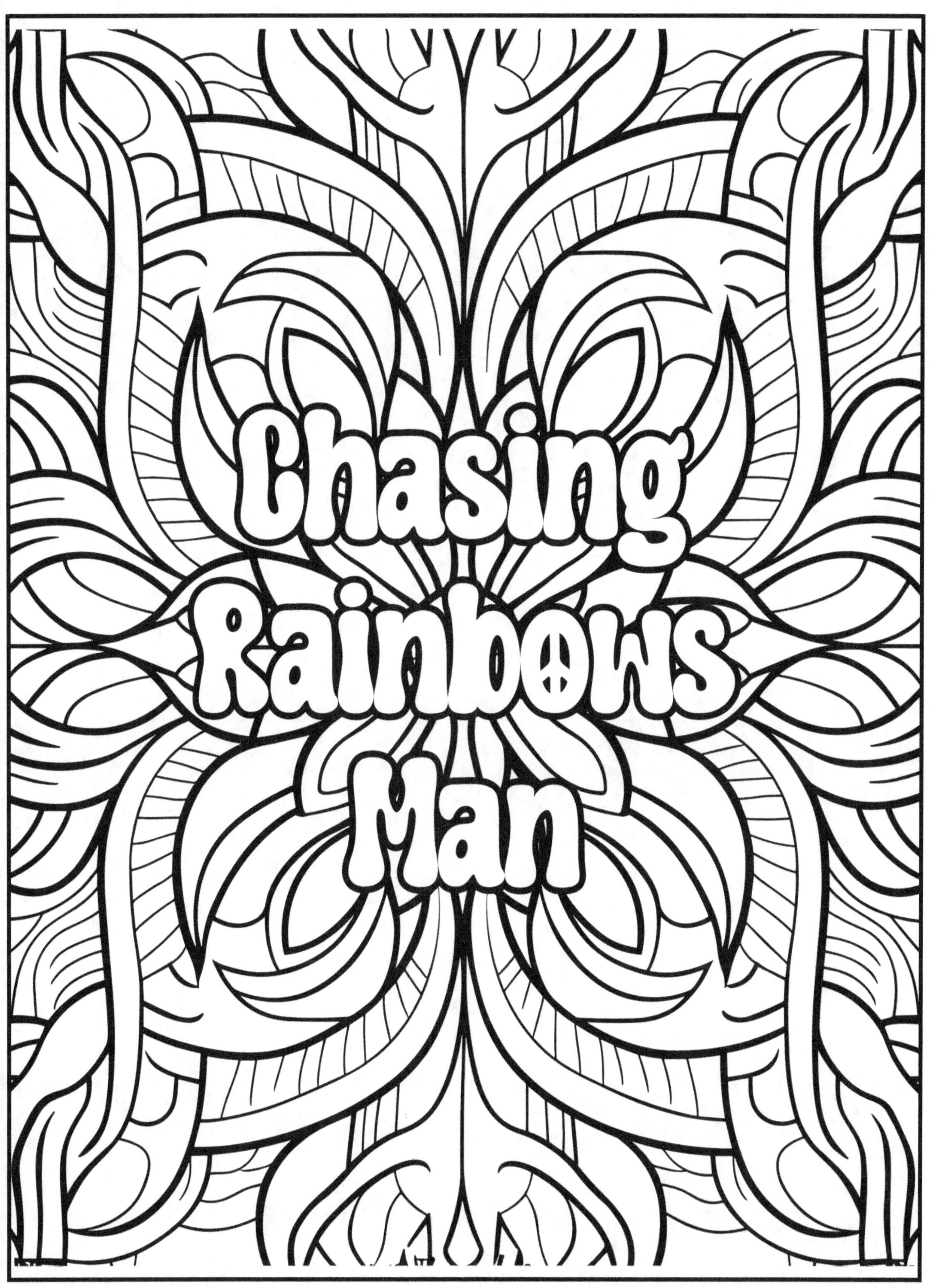

Chasing
Rainbows
Man

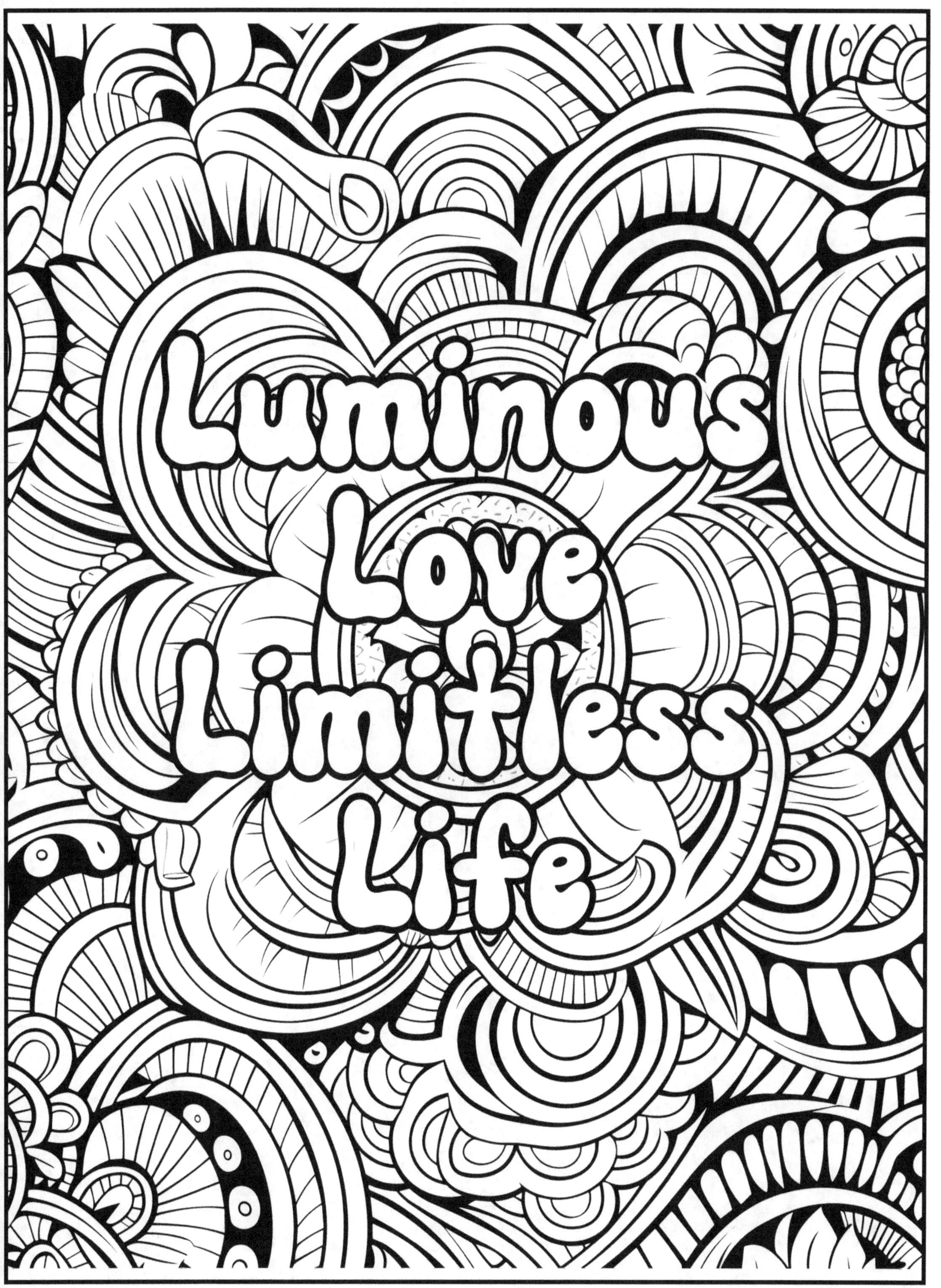

Luminous
Love
Limitless
Life

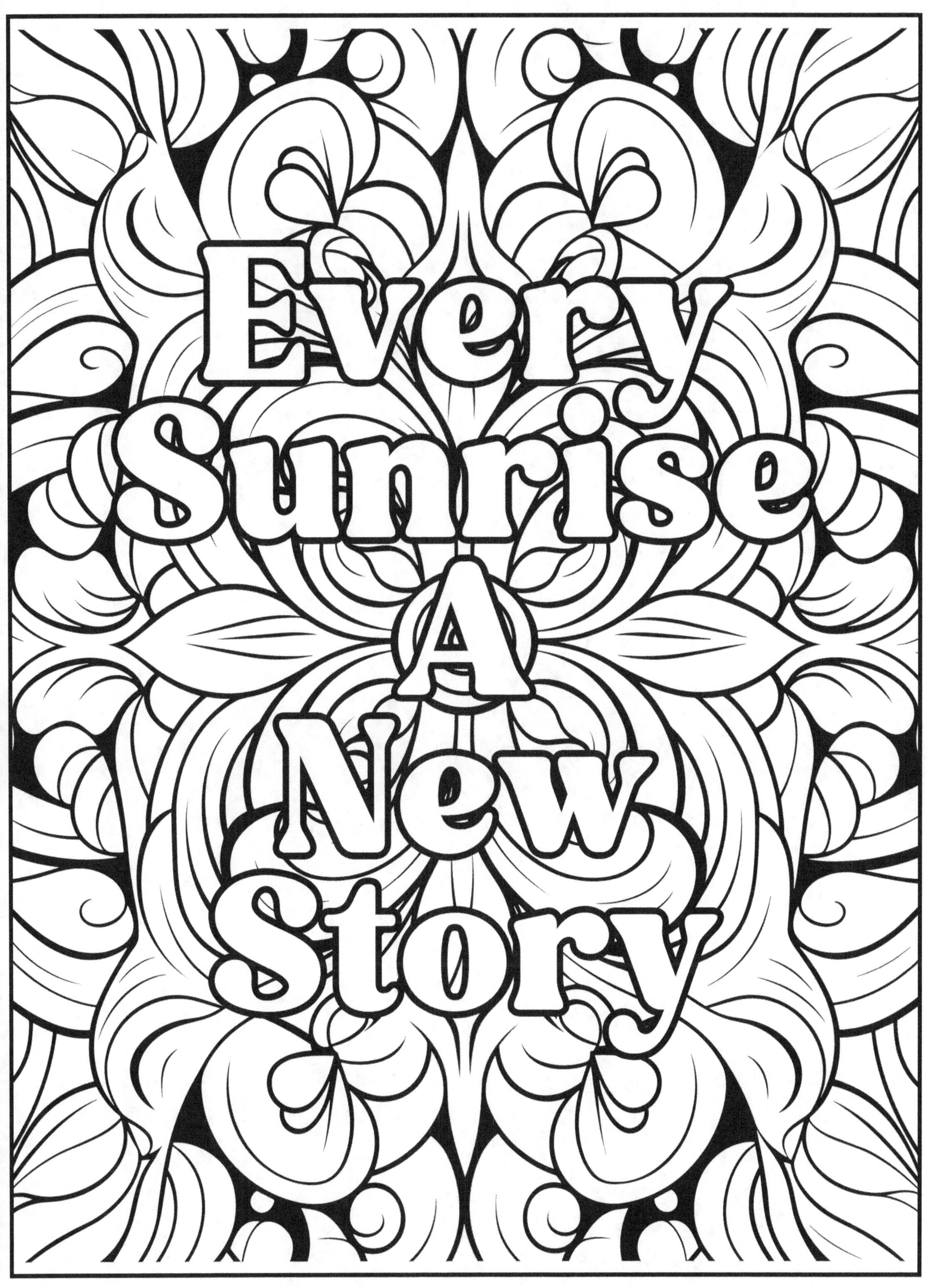

Every
Sunrise
A
New
Story

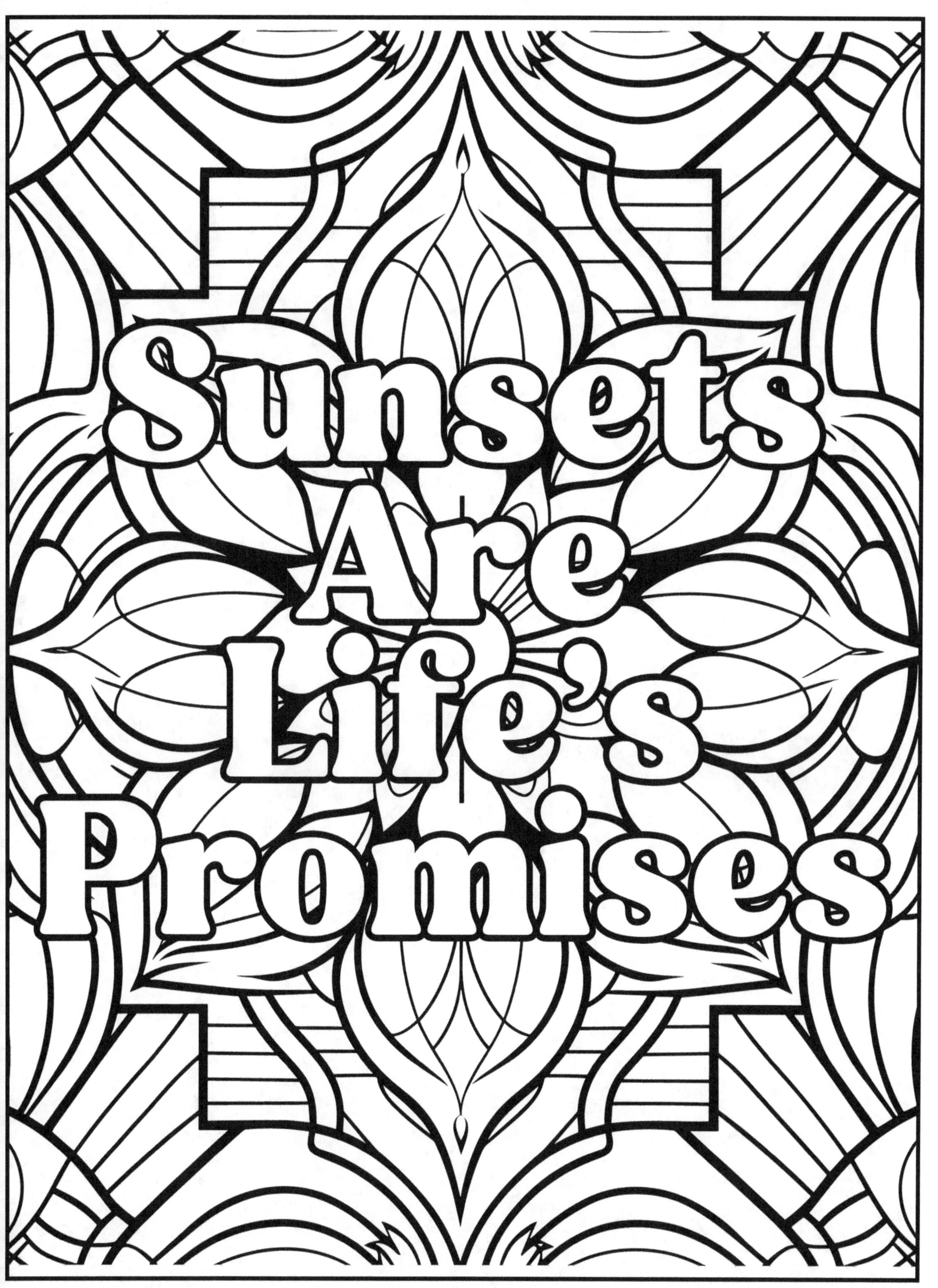

Sunsets
Are
Life's
Promises

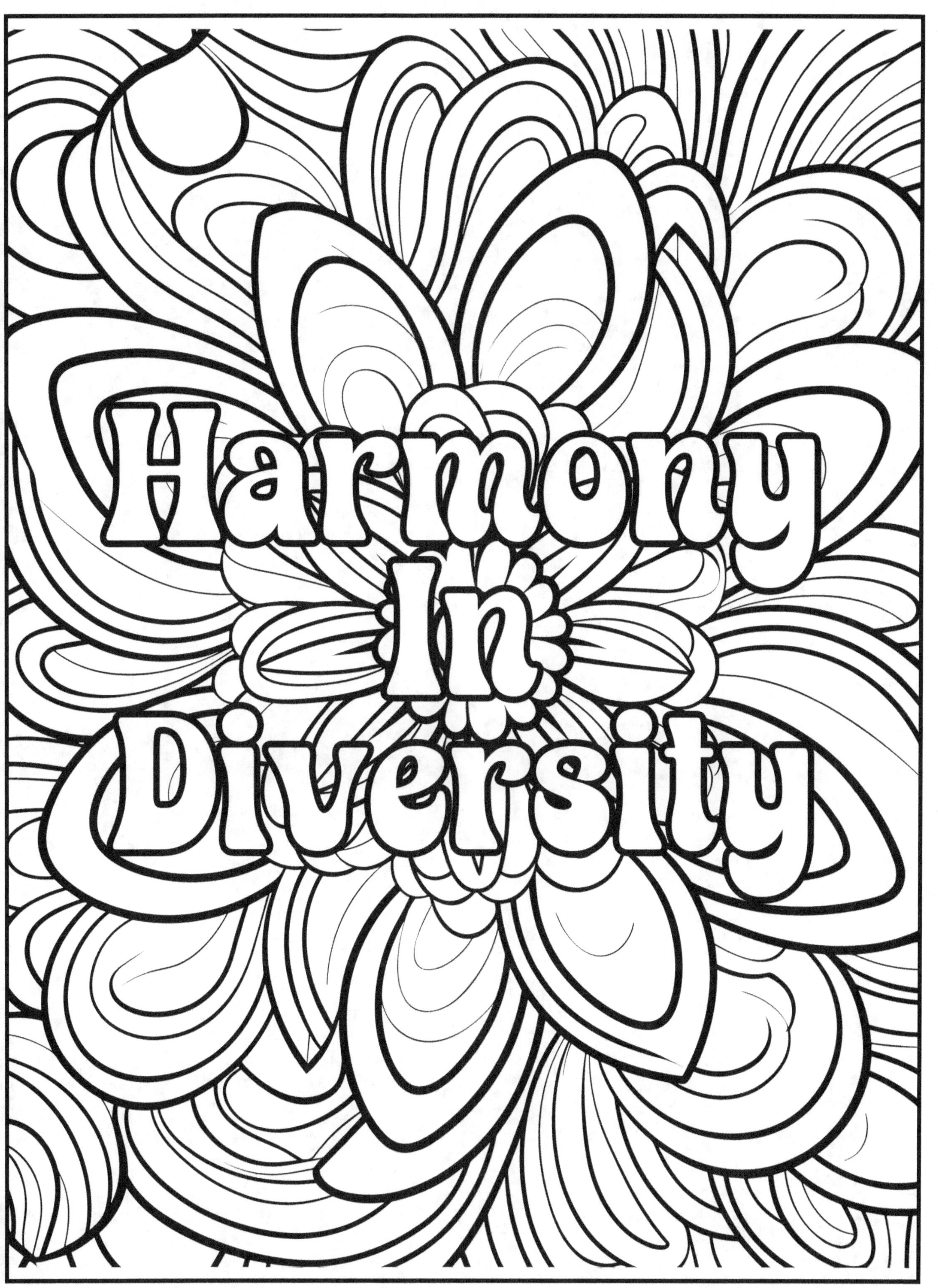
Harmony In Diversity

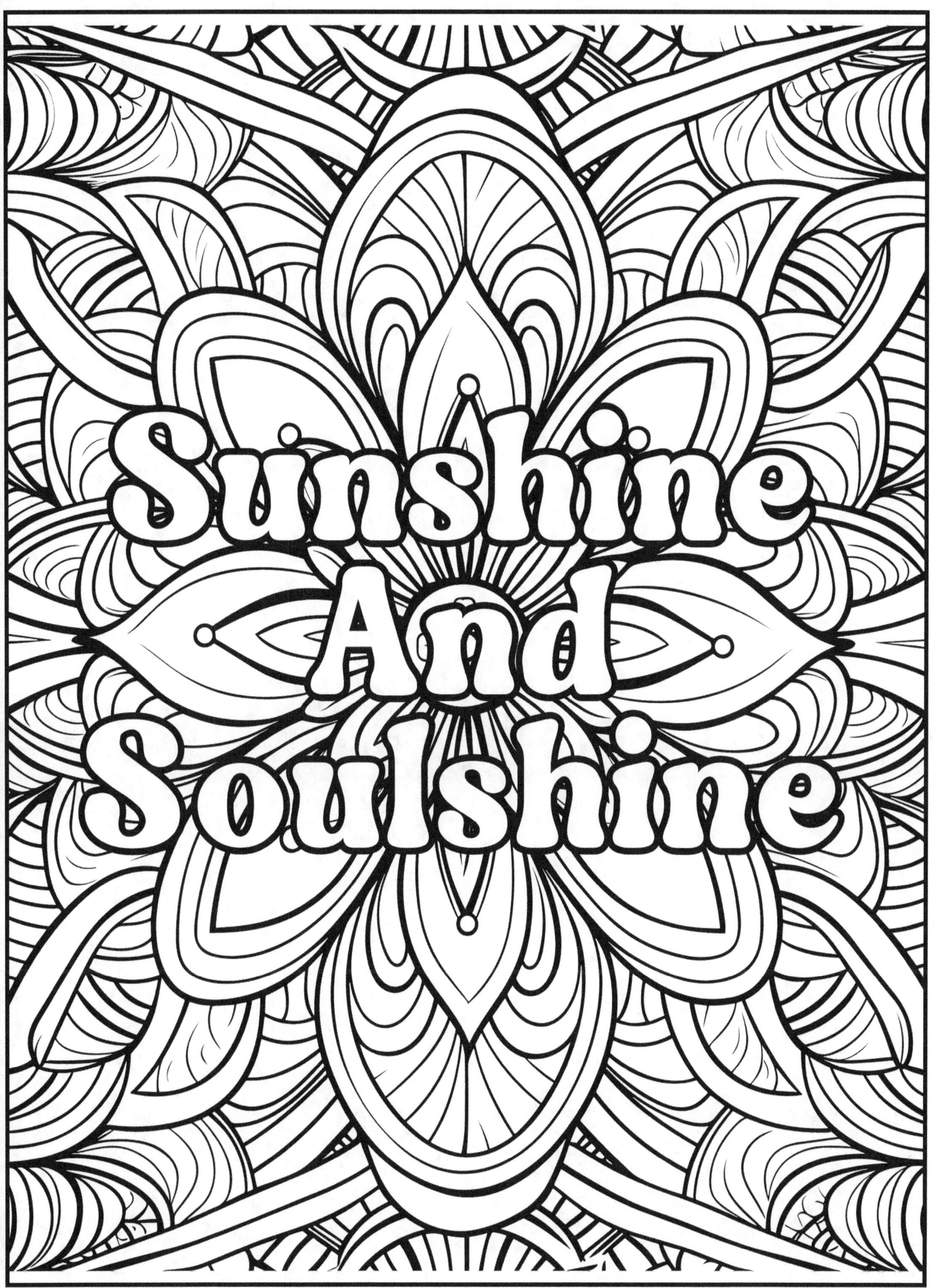
Sunshine
And
Soulshine

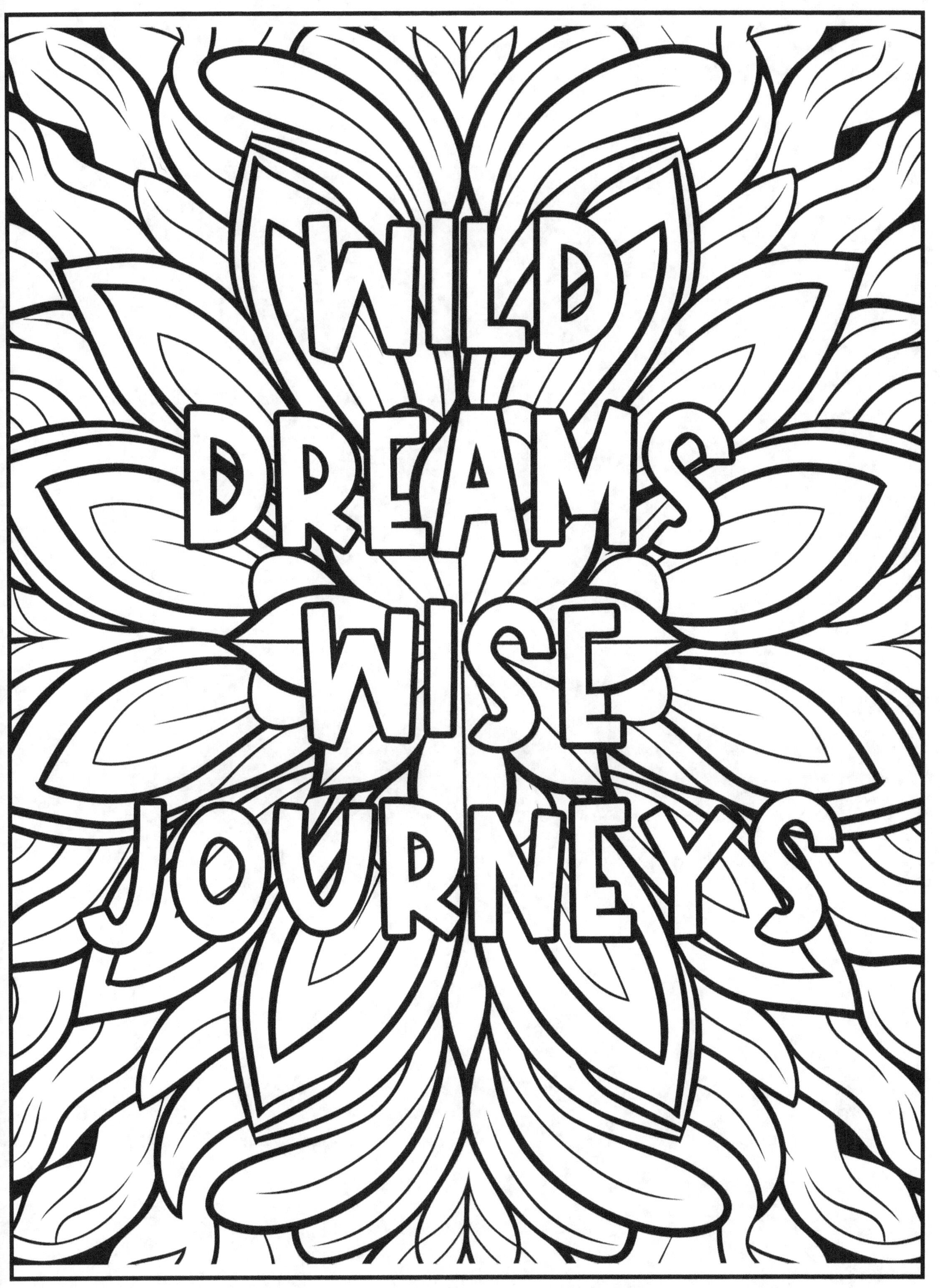
WILD
DREAMS
WISE
JOURNEYS

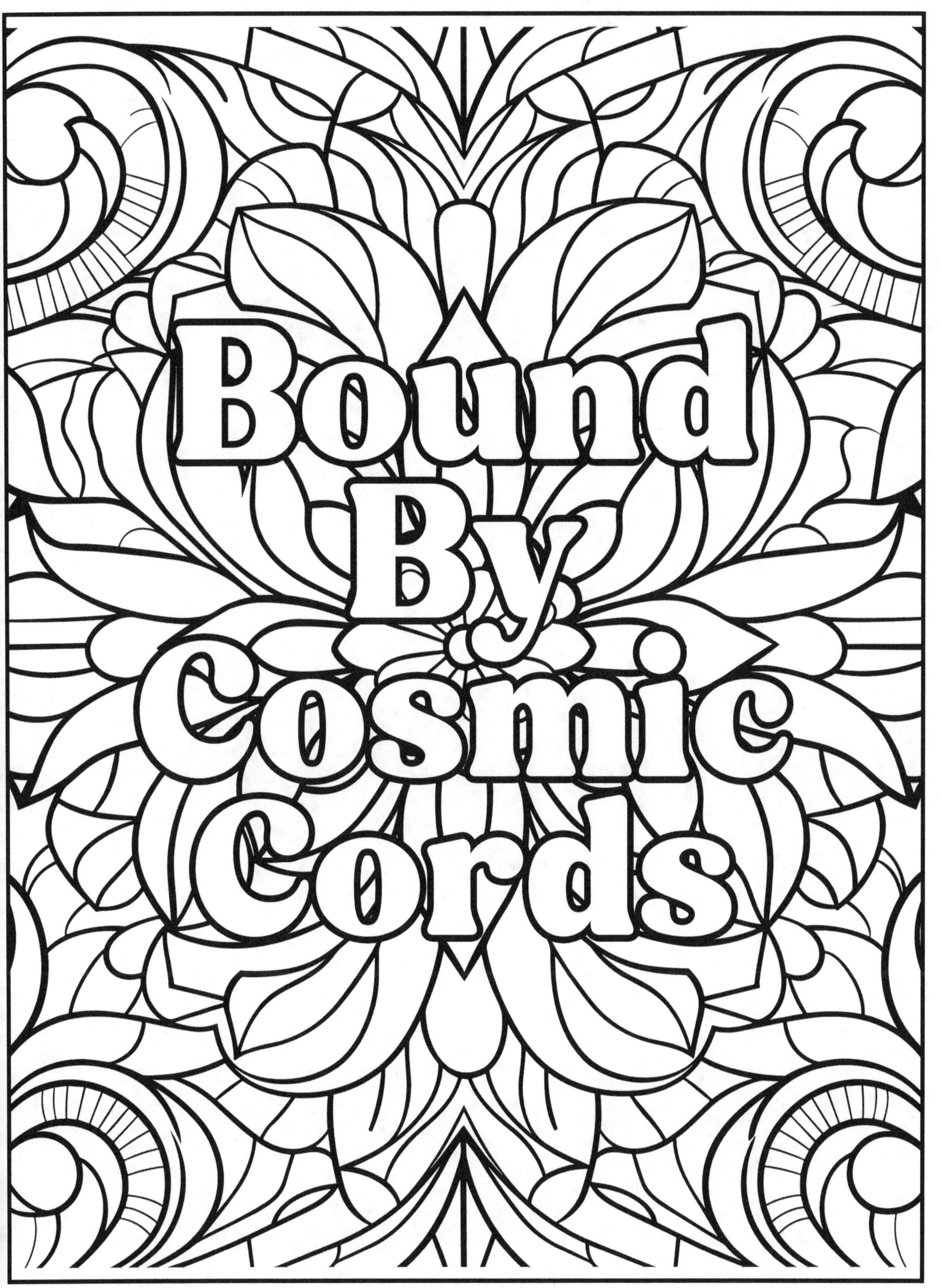

Bound
By
Cosmic
Cords

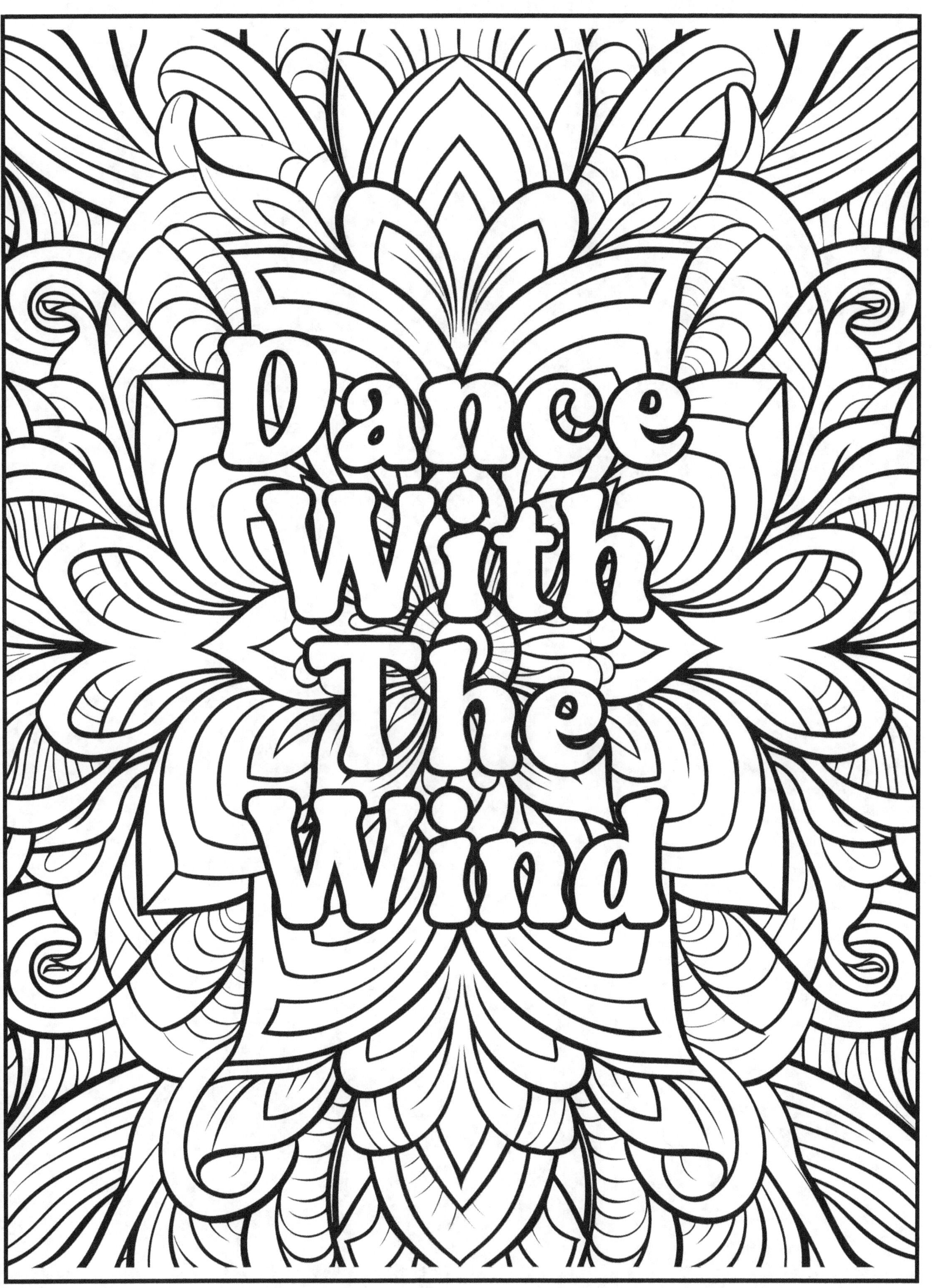

Dance
With
The
Wind

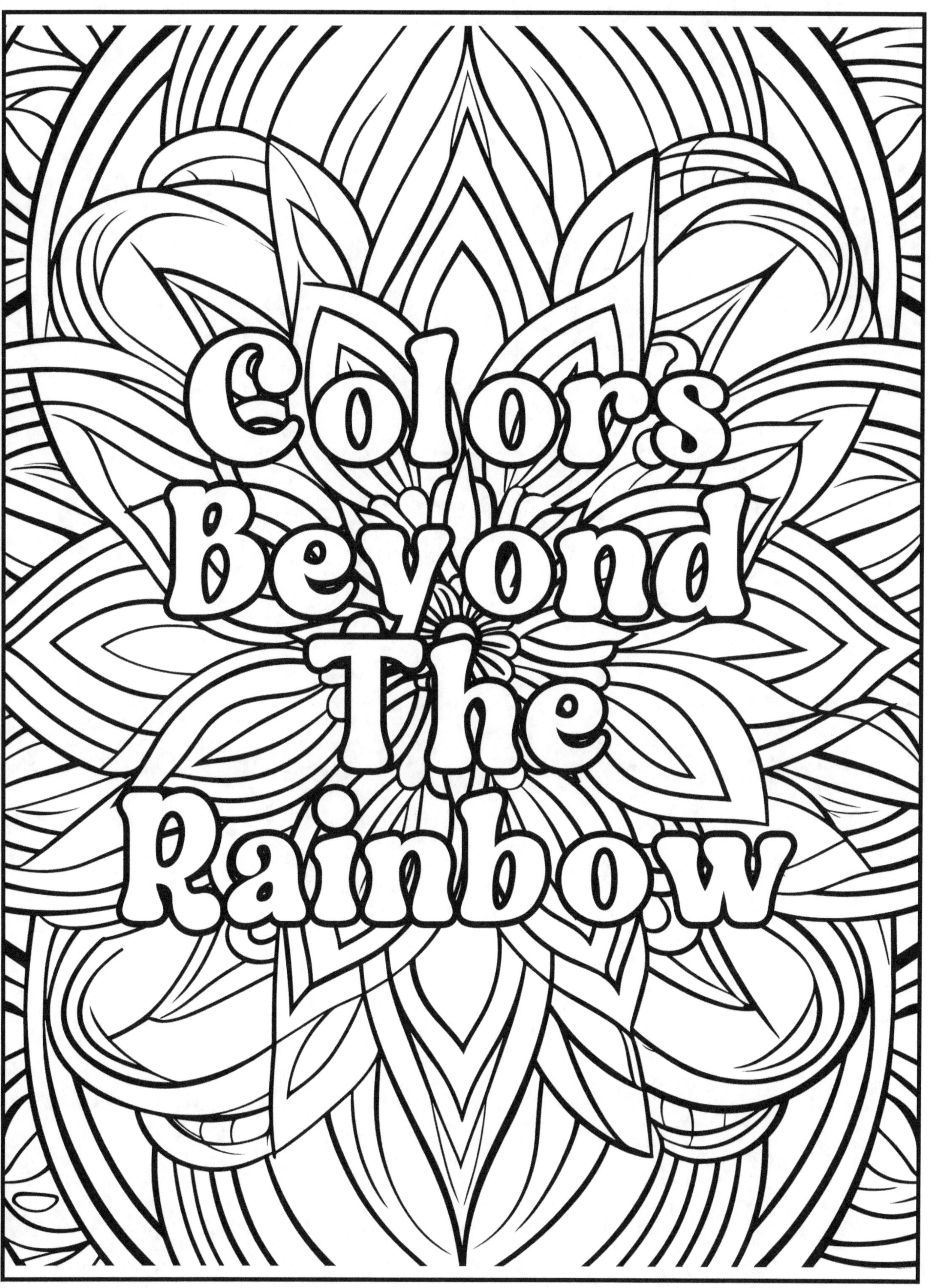

Colors
Beyond
The
Rainbow

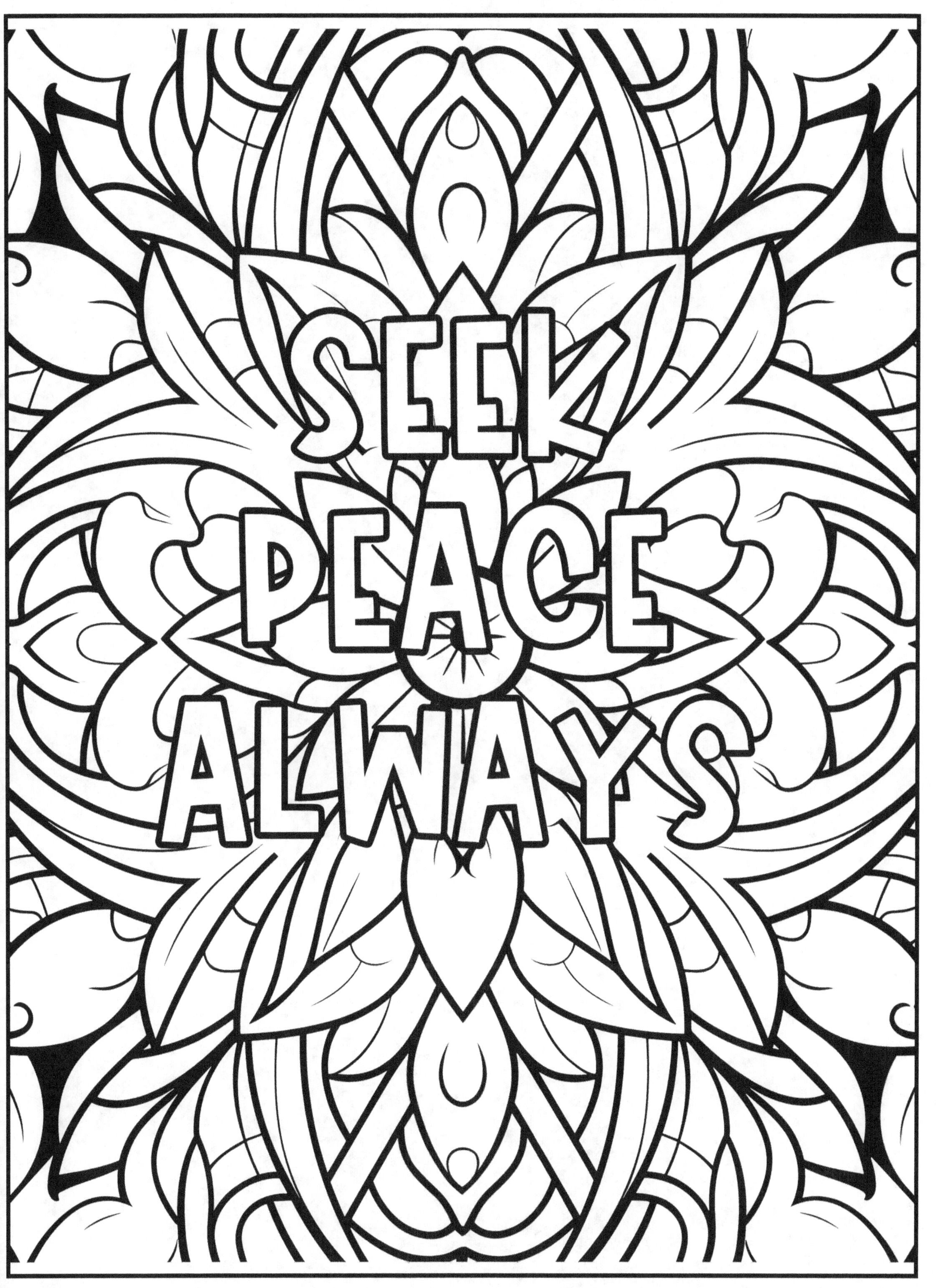

SEEK
PEACE
ALWAYS

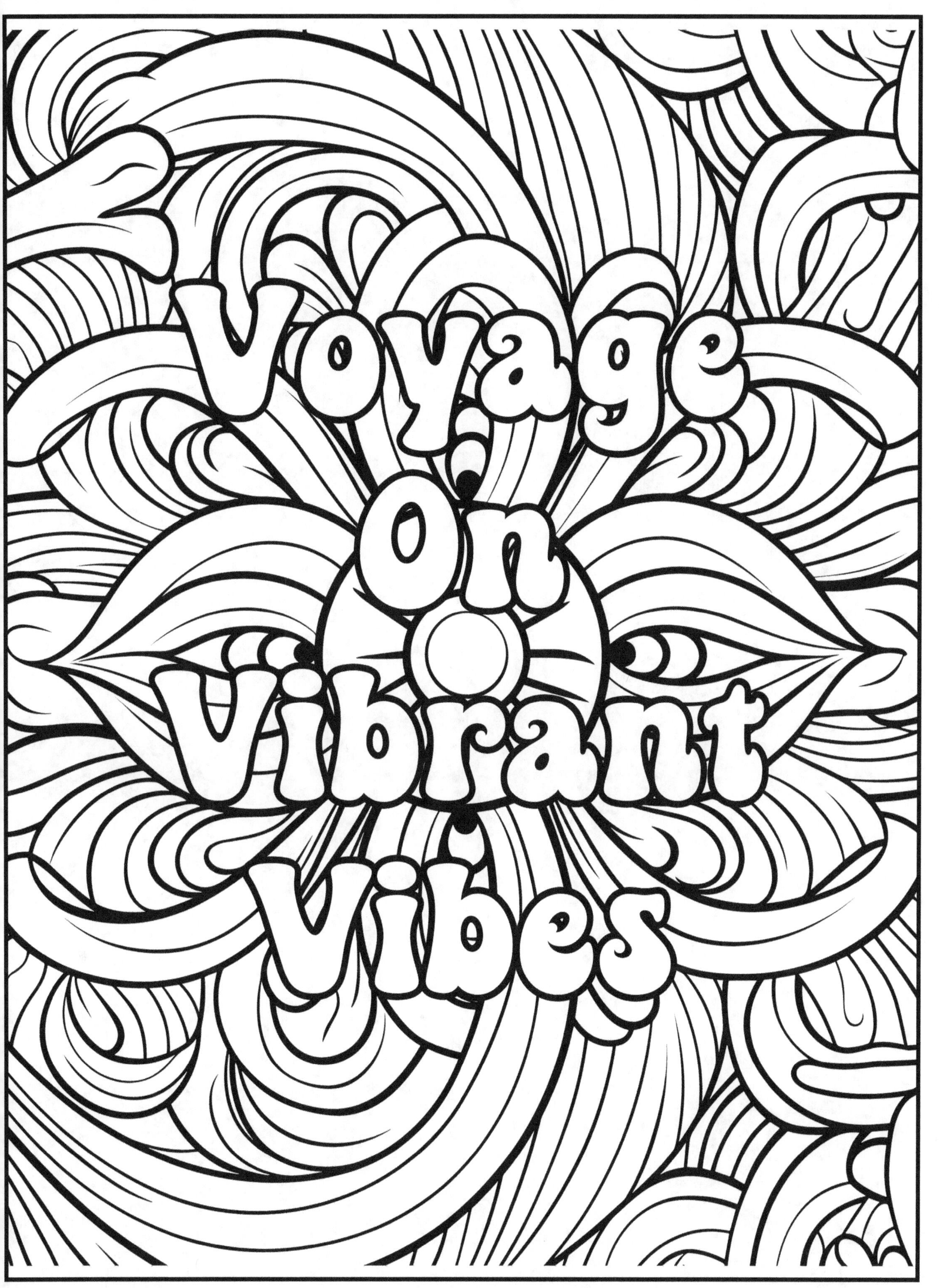
Voyage On Vibrant Vibes

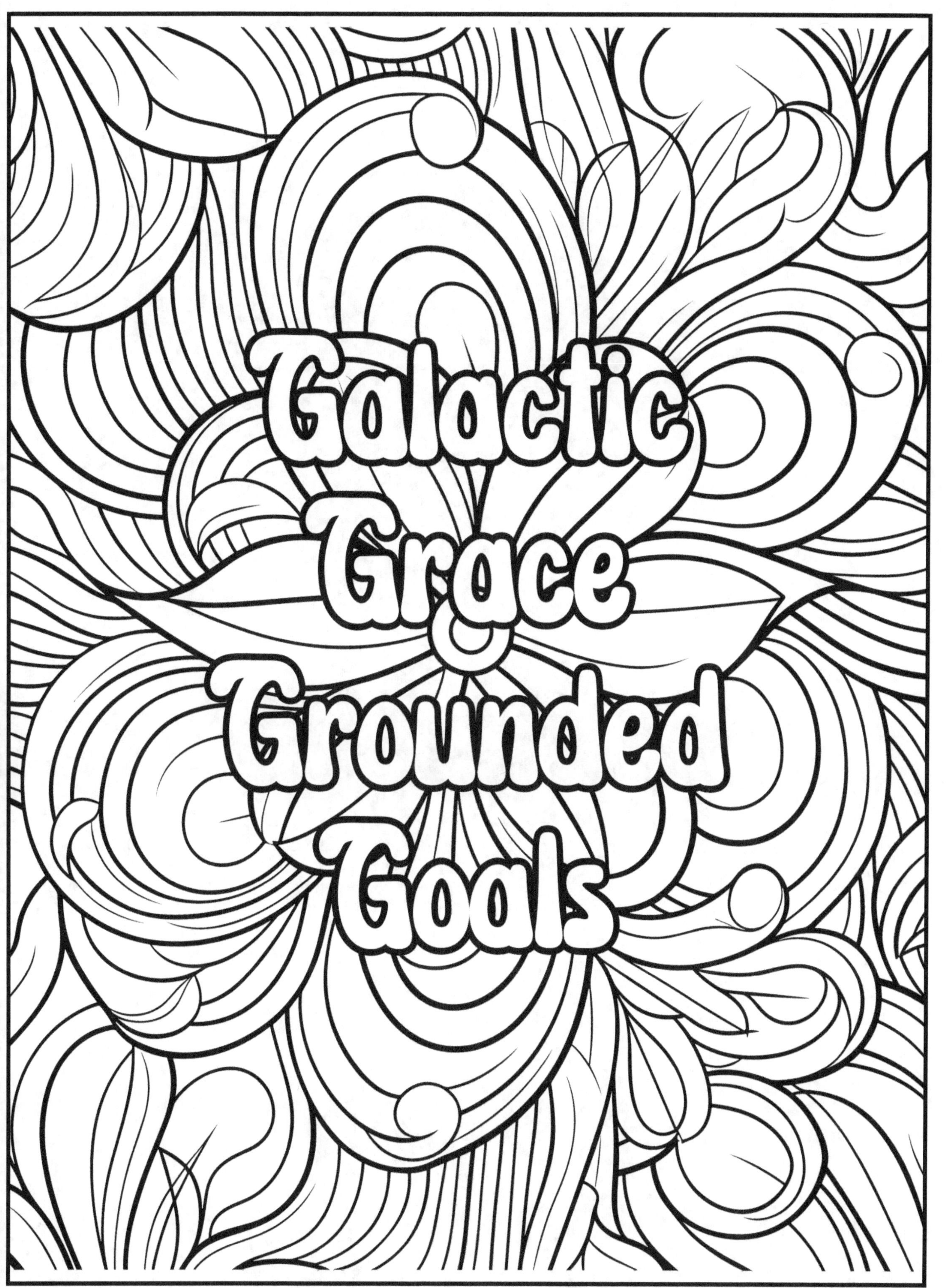

Galactic
Grace
Grounded
Goals

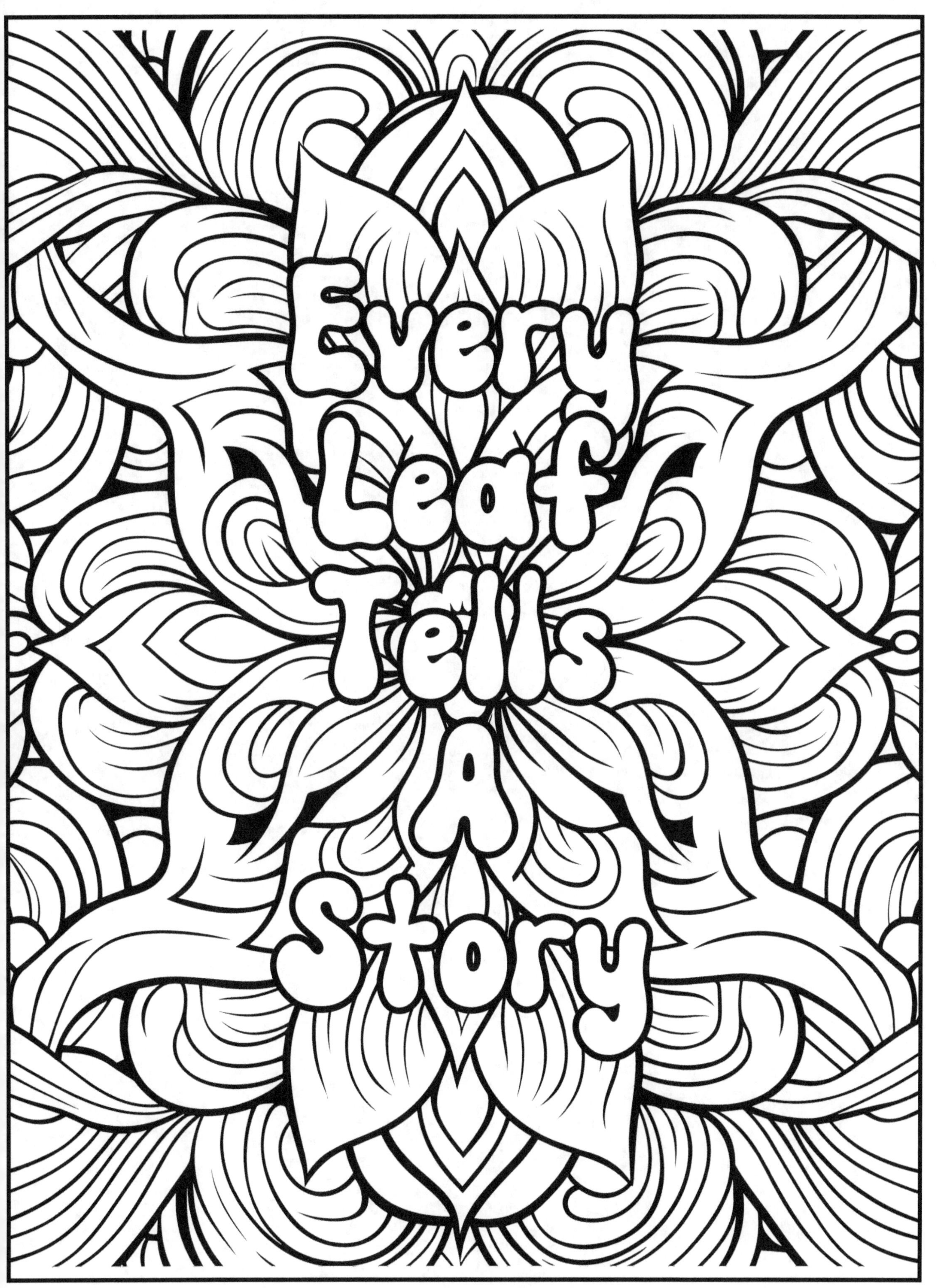

Every
Leaf
Tells
A
Story

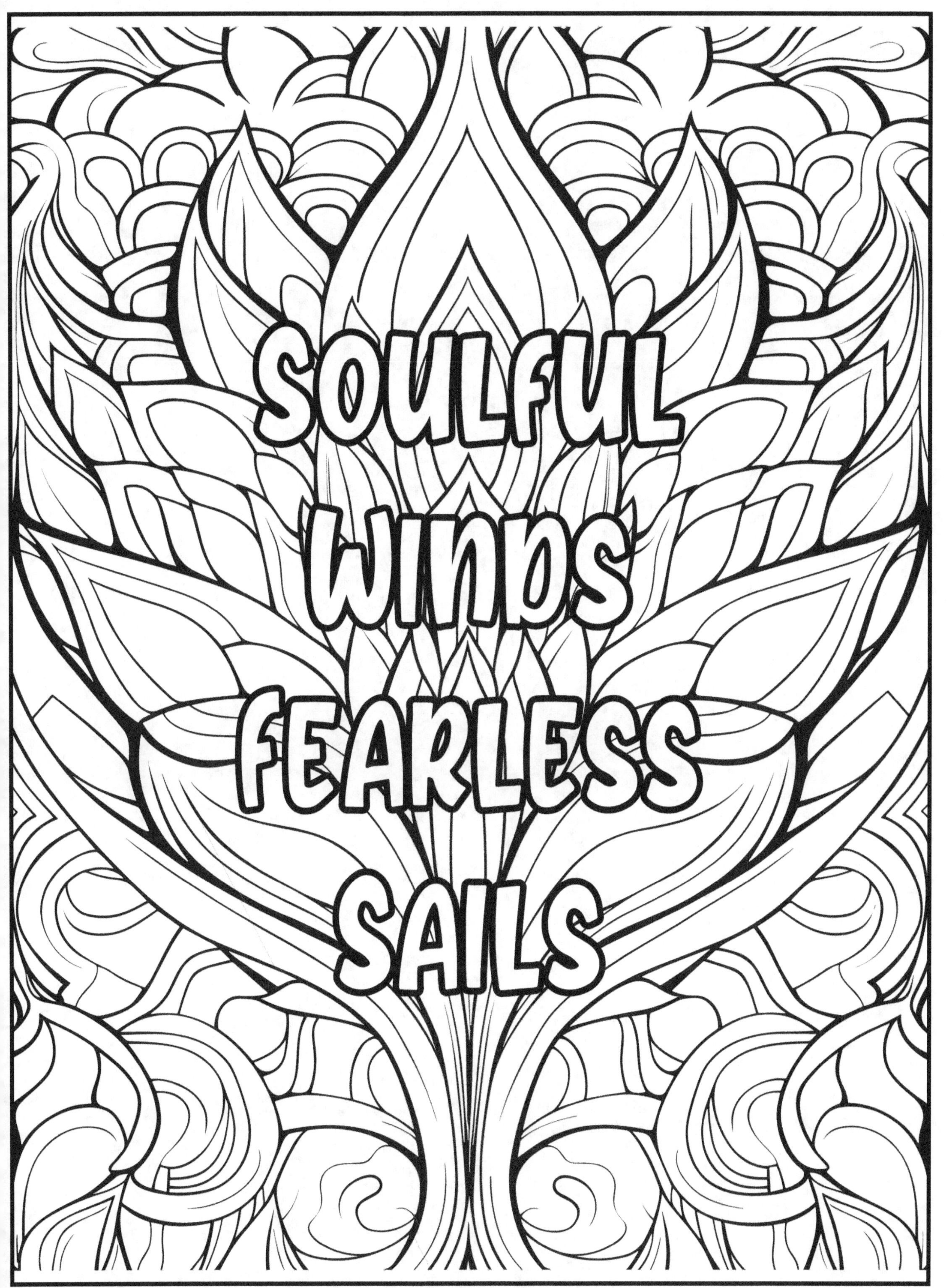

SOULFUL
WINDS
FEARLESS
SAILS

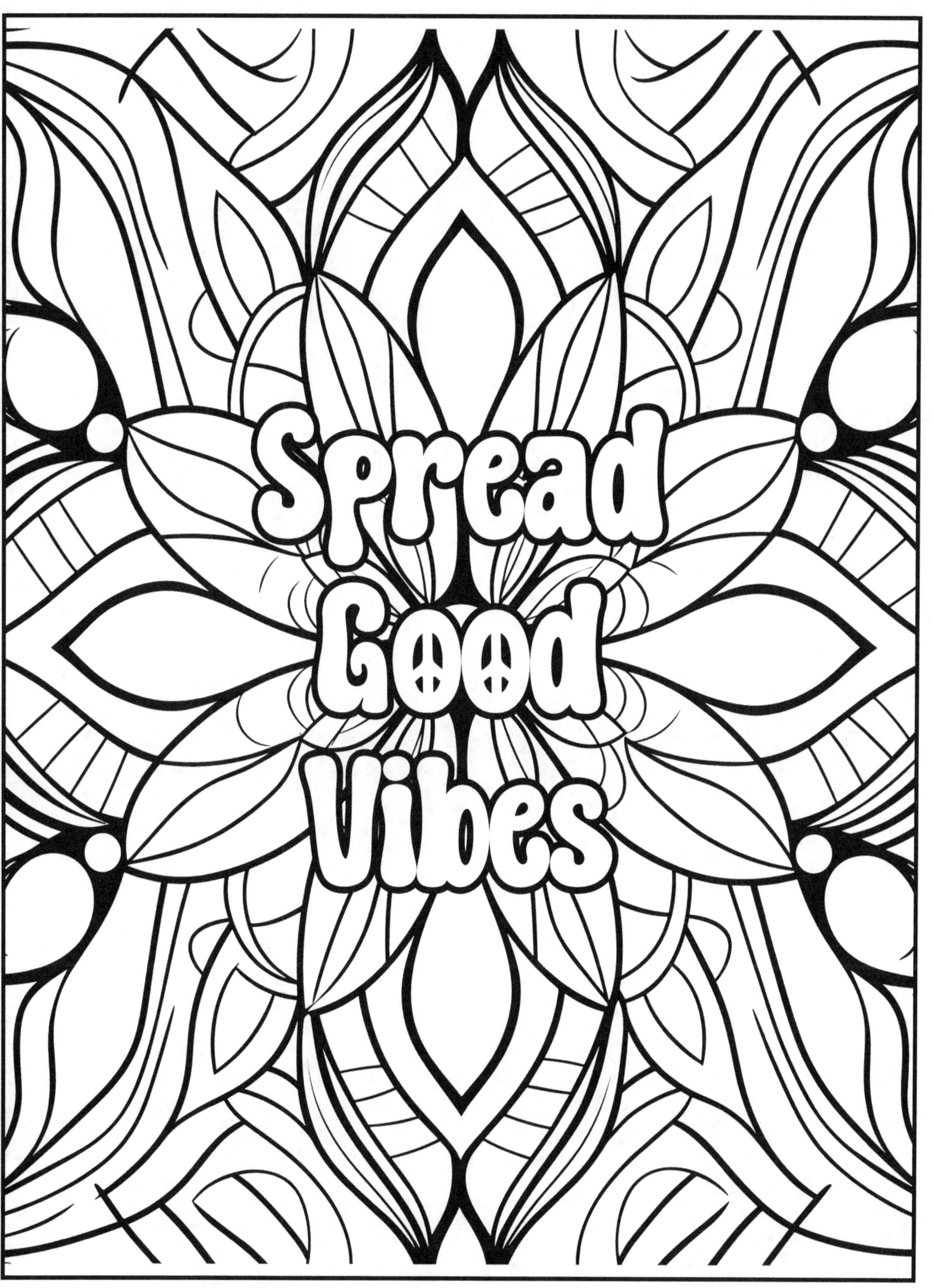

Spread
Good
Vibes

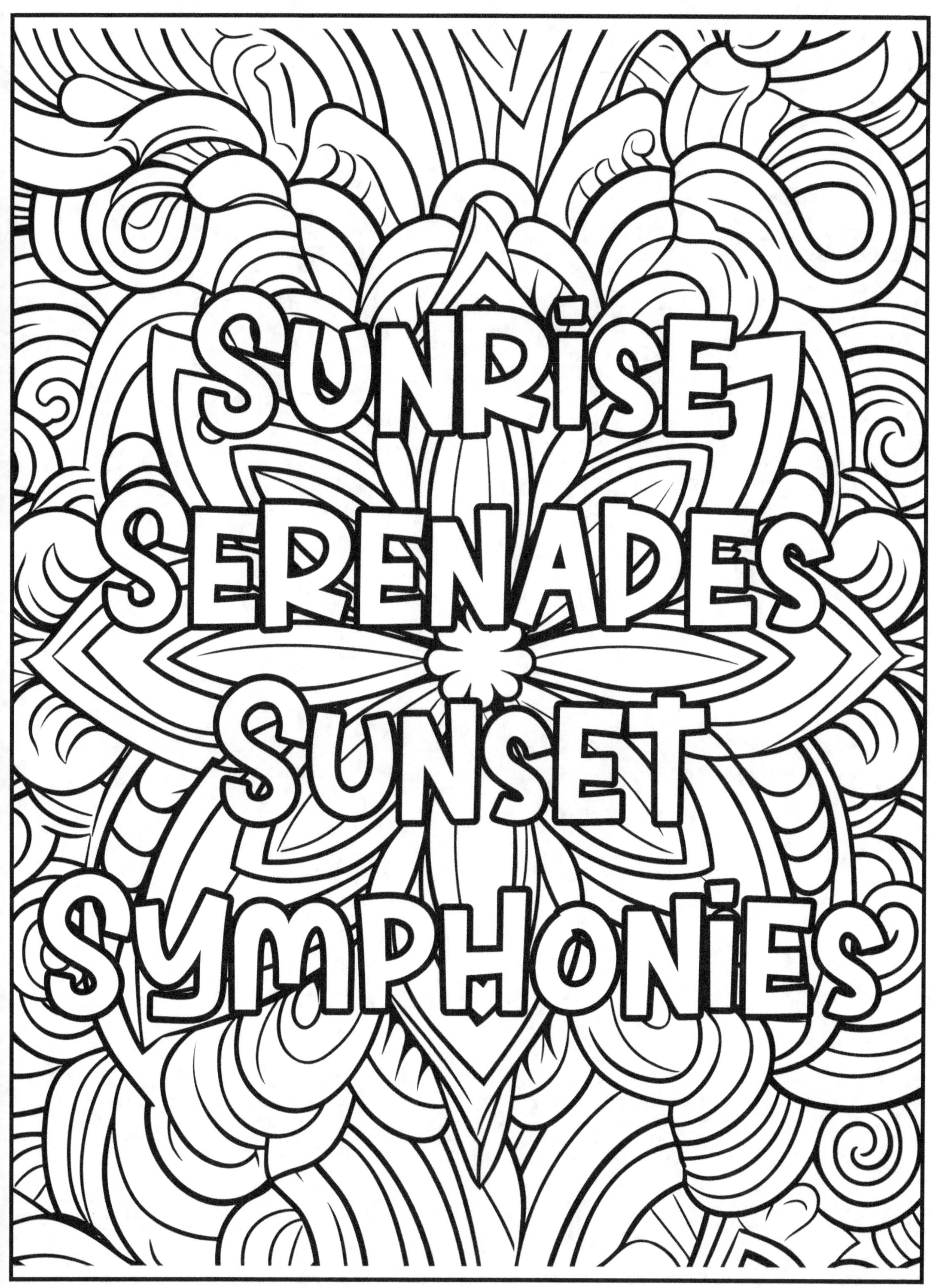
SUNRISE
SERENADES
SUNSET
SYMPHONIES

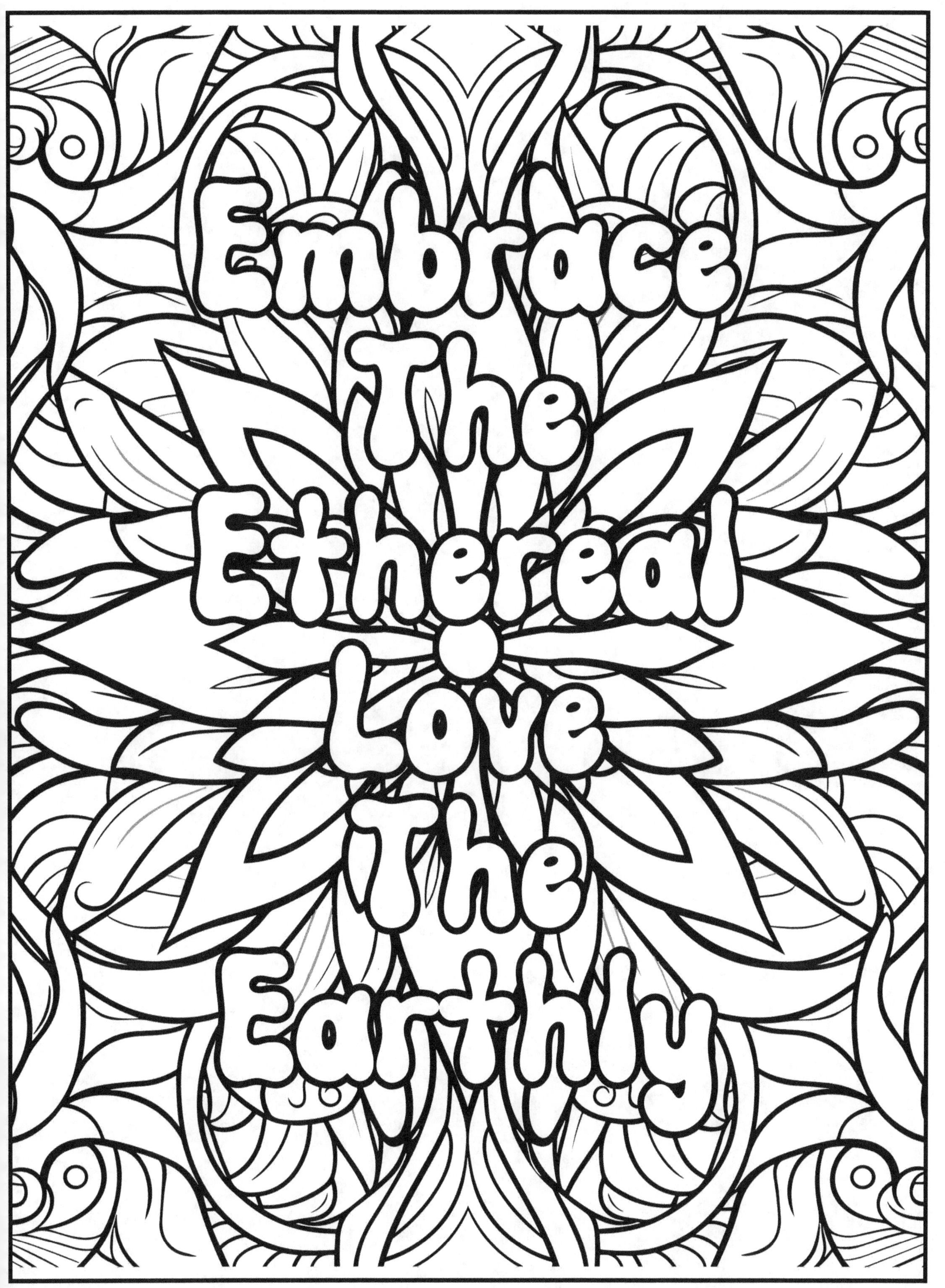
Embrace The Ethereal Love The Earthly

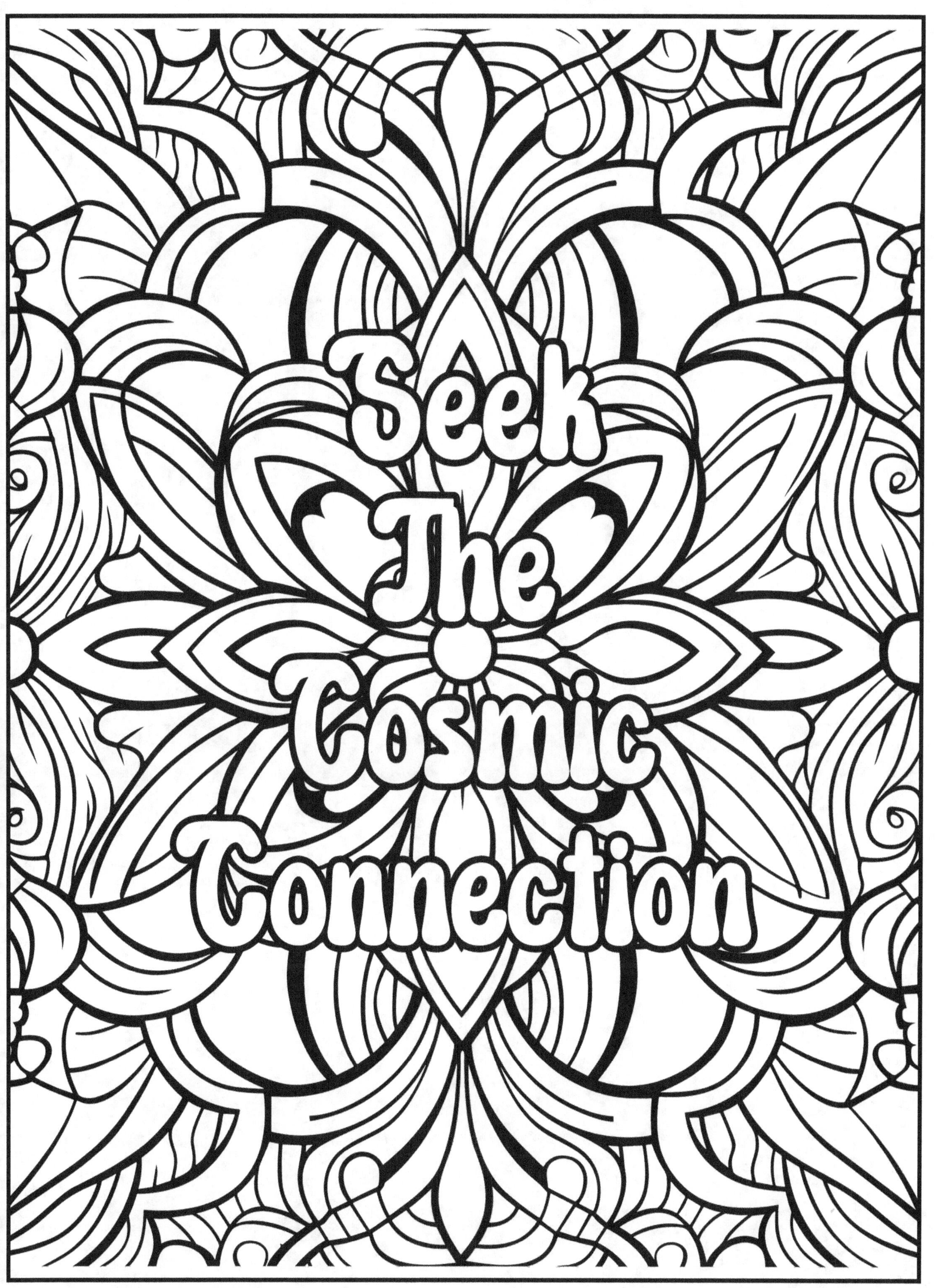

Seek
The
Cosmic
Connection

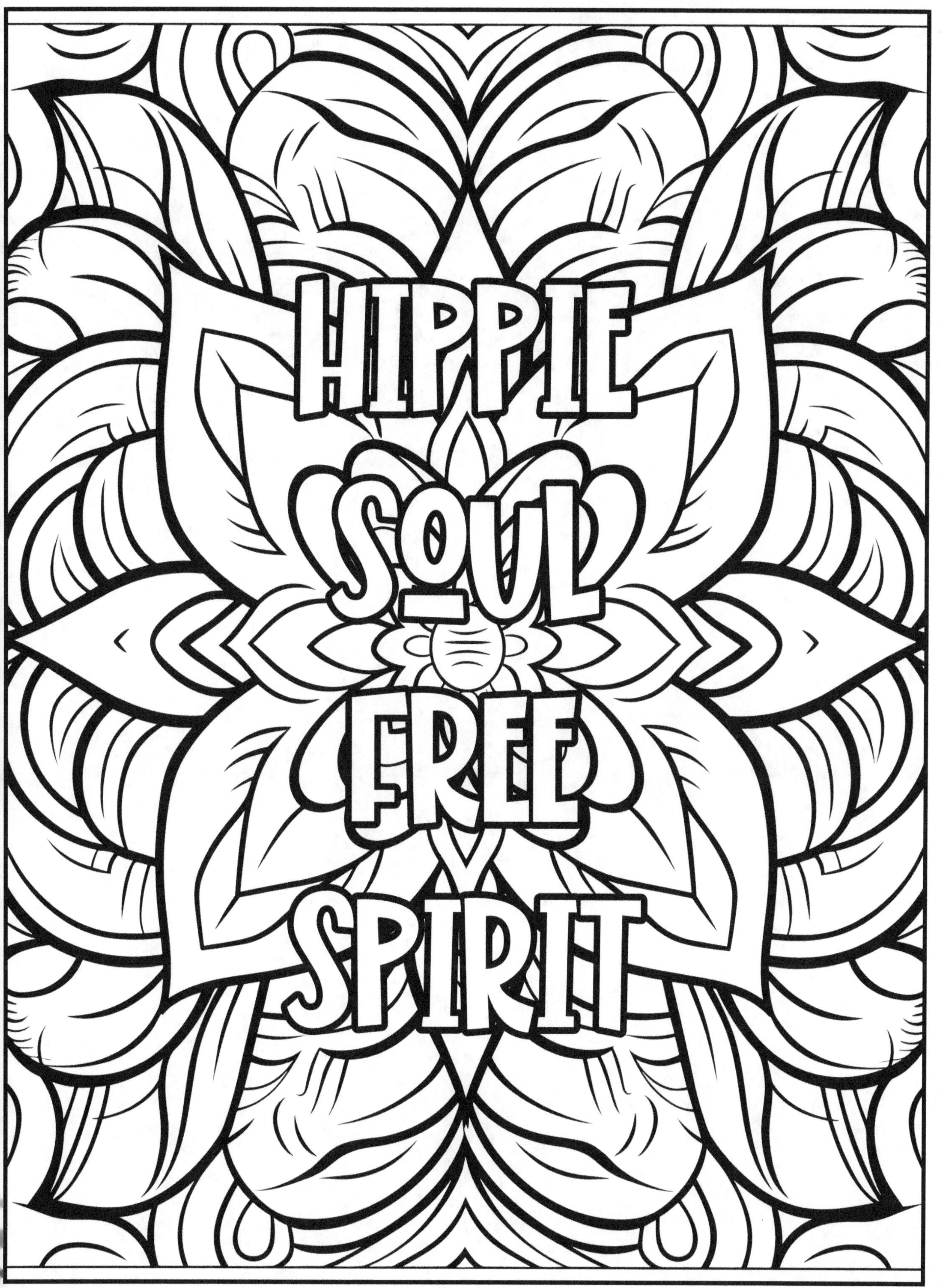

HIPPIE
SOUL
FREE
SPIRIT

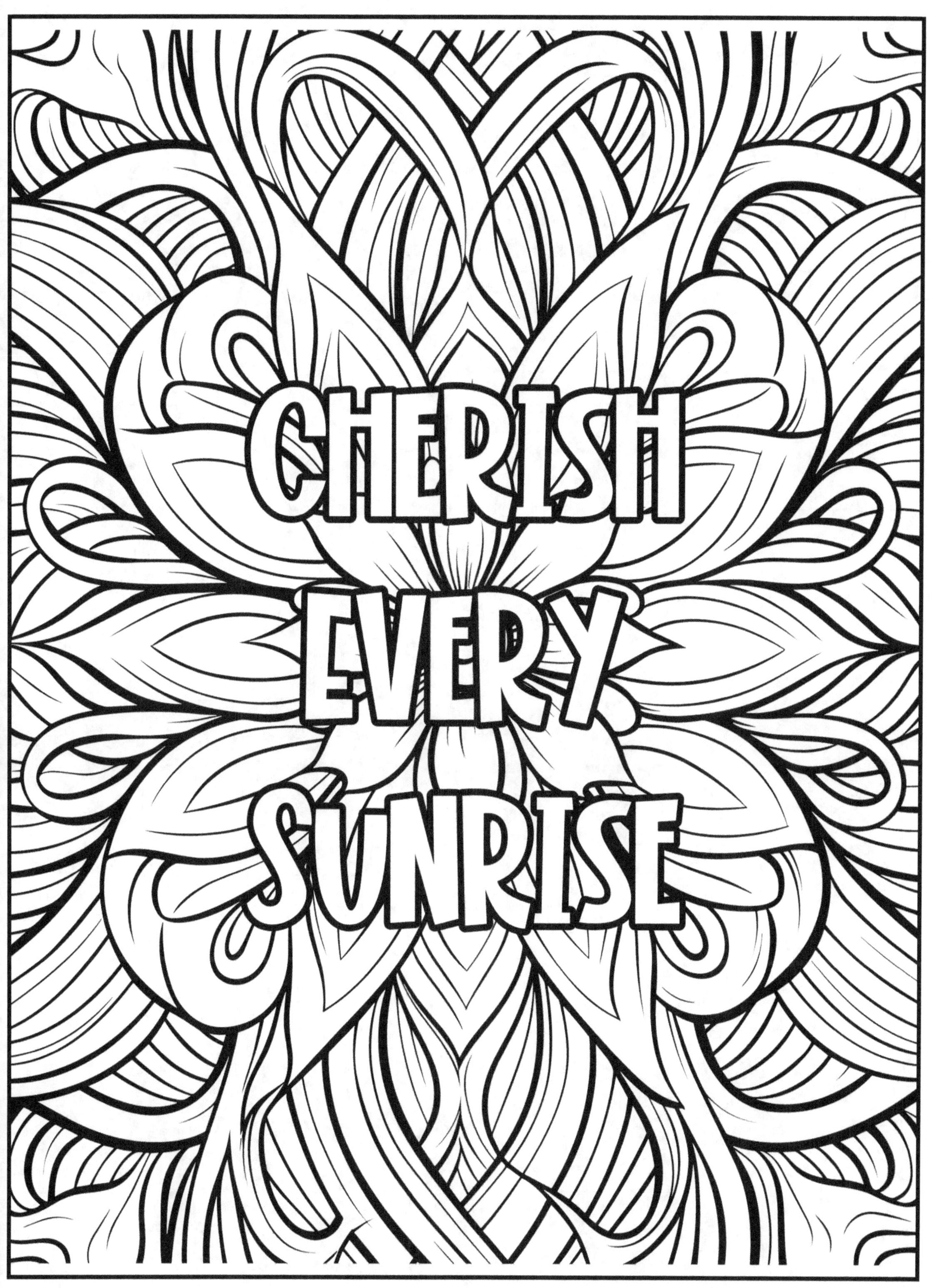

CHERISH
EVERY
SUNRISE

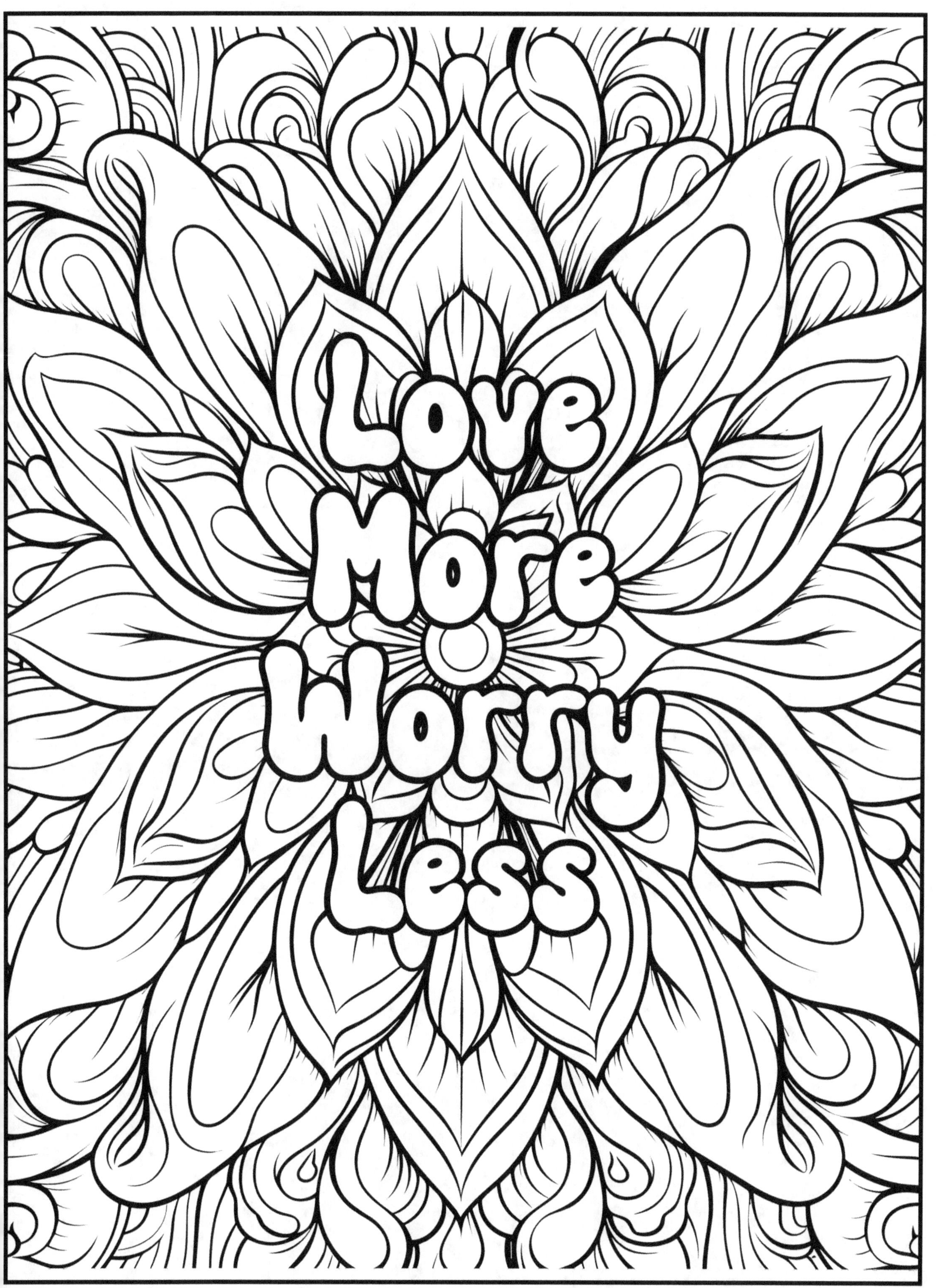
Love
More
Worry
Less

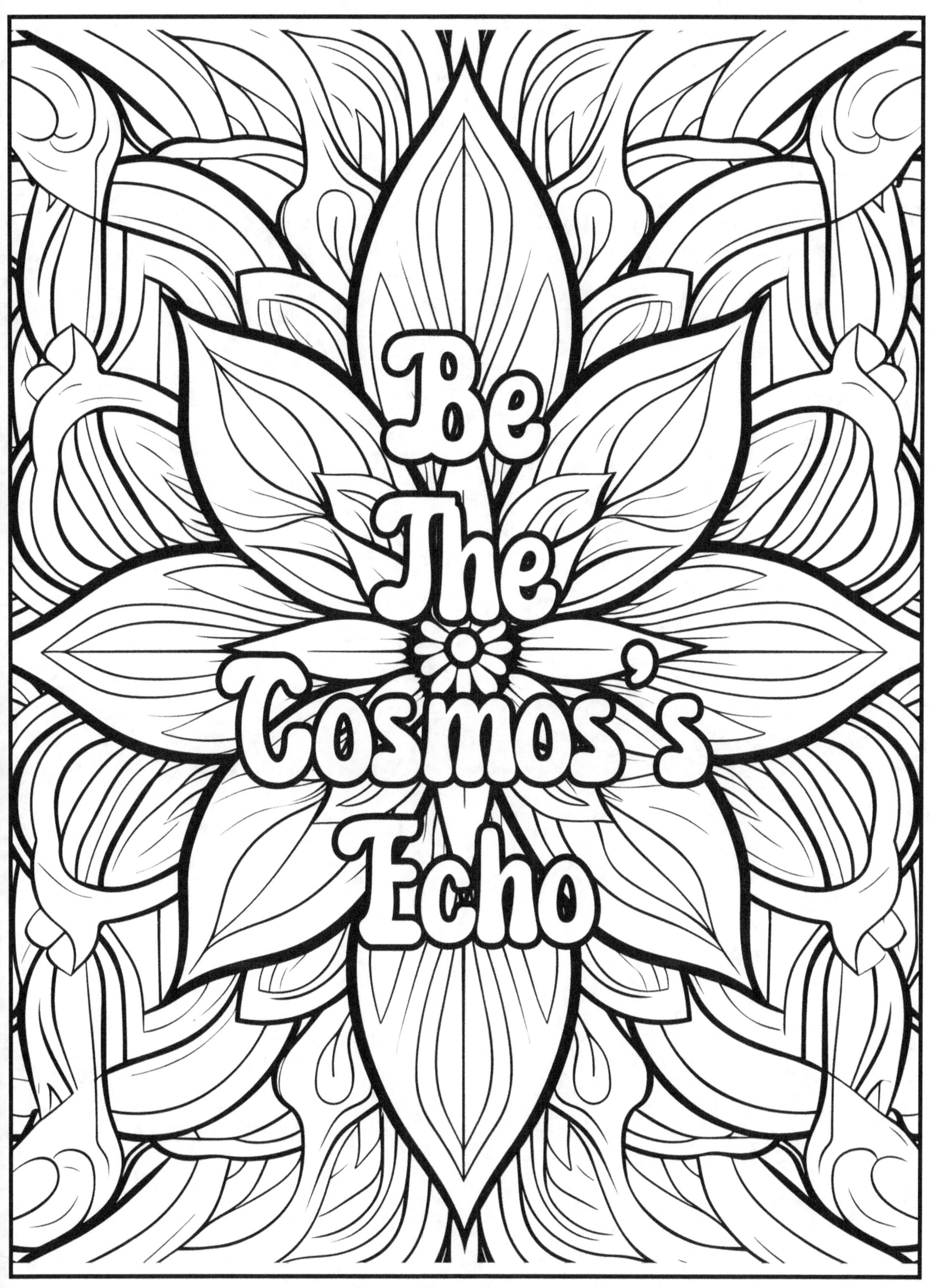
Be
The
Cosmos's
Echo

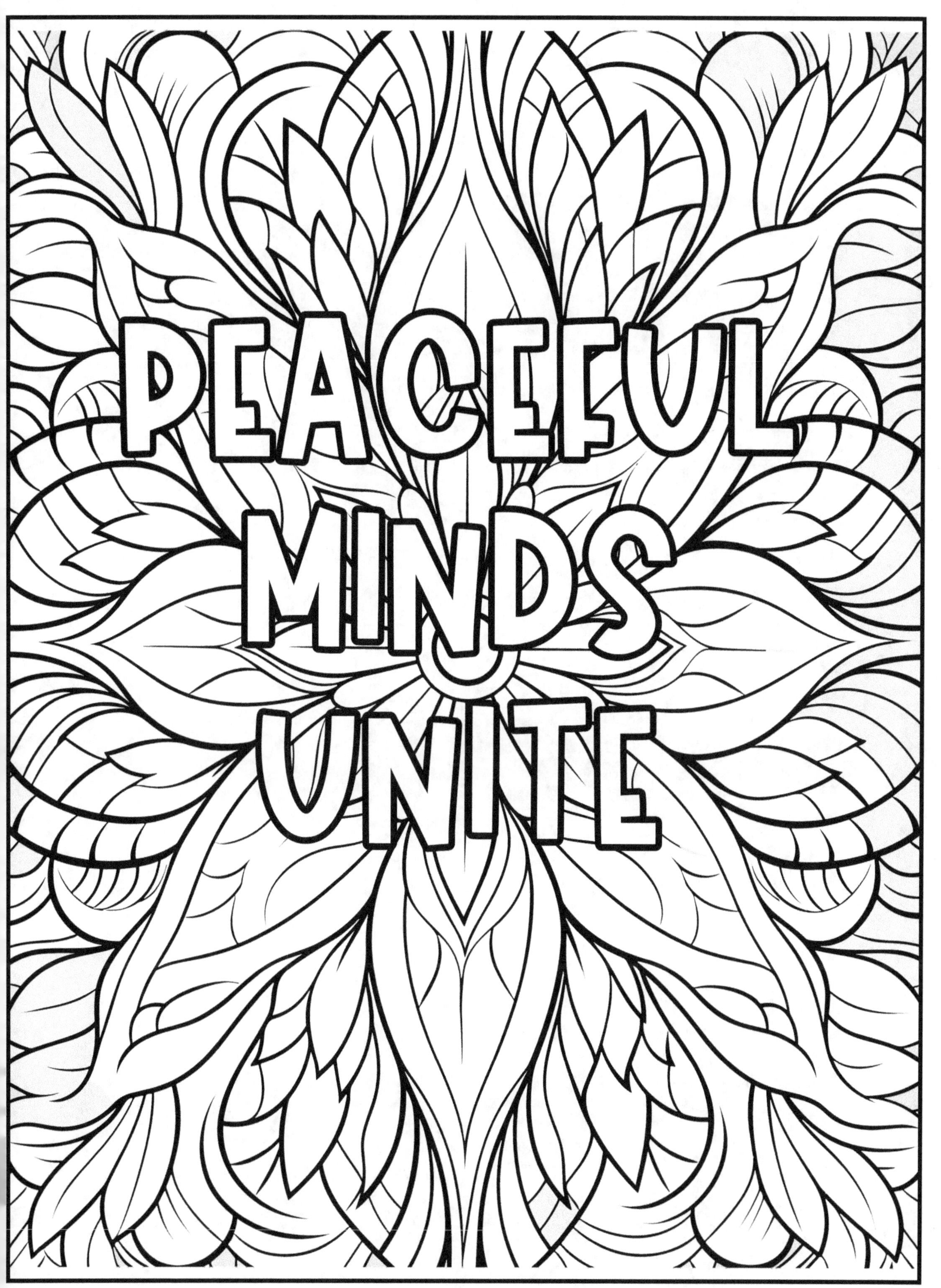

PEACEFUL
MINDS
UNITE

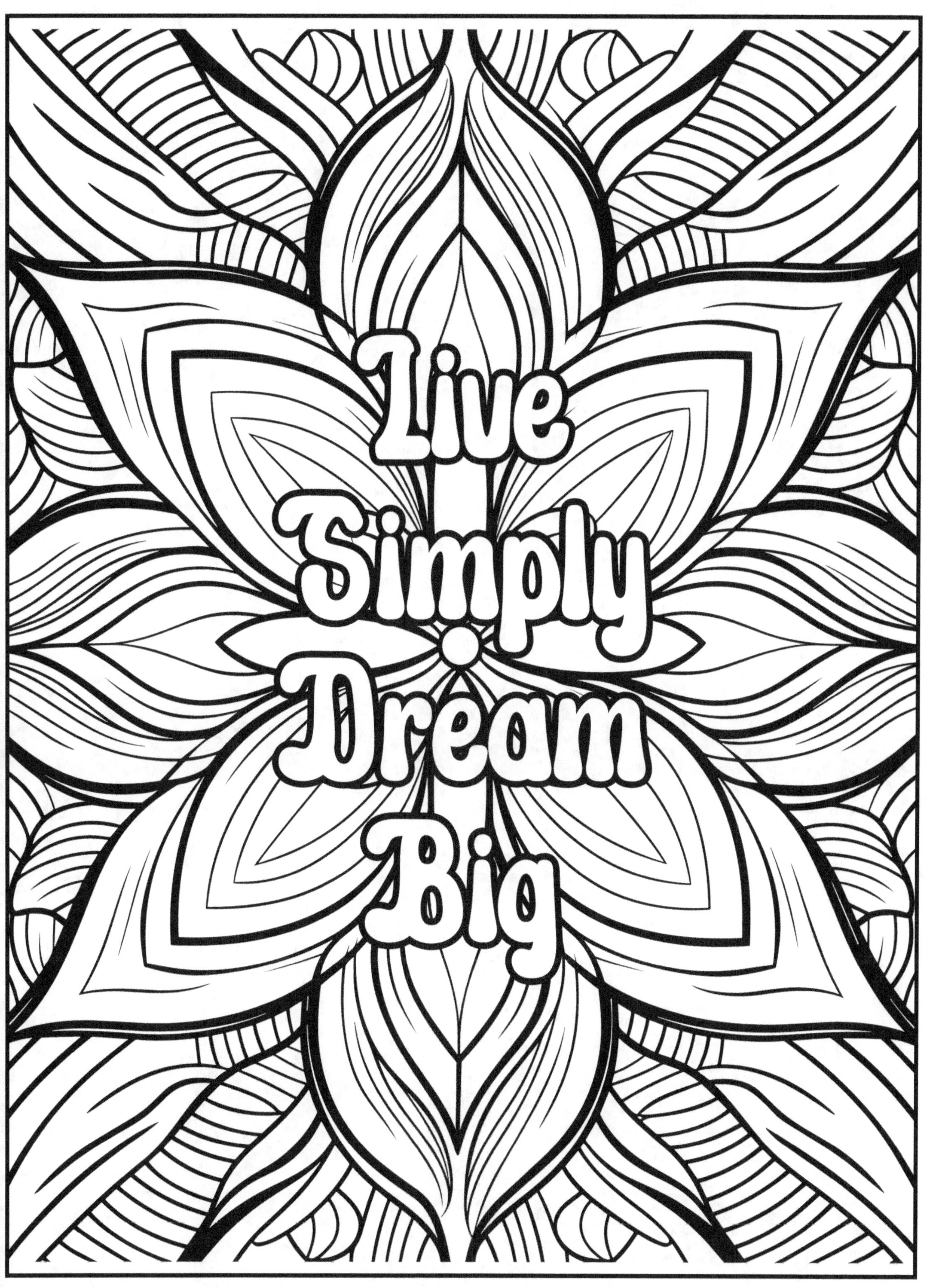
Live
Simply
Dream
Big

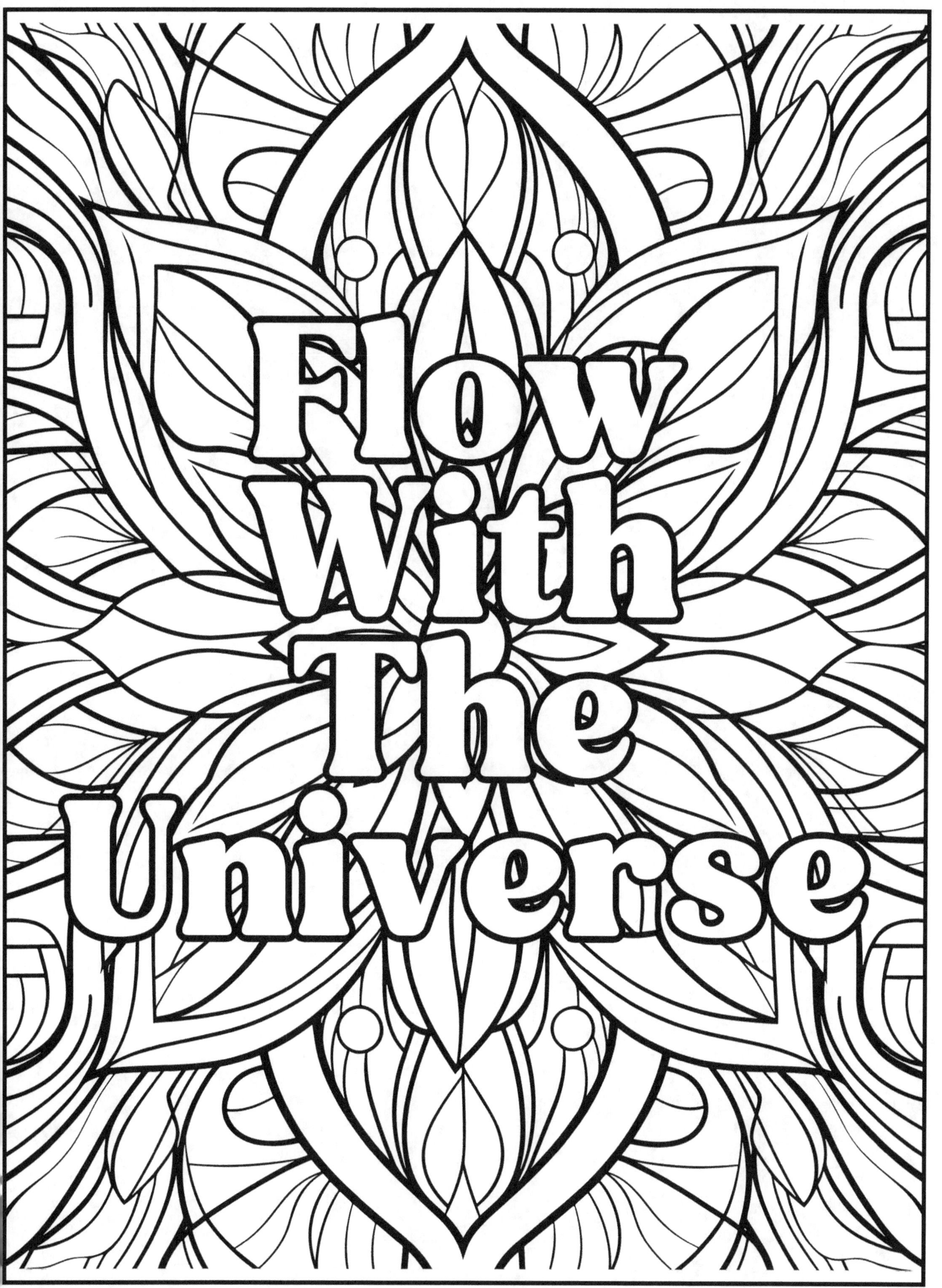
Flow
With
The
Universe

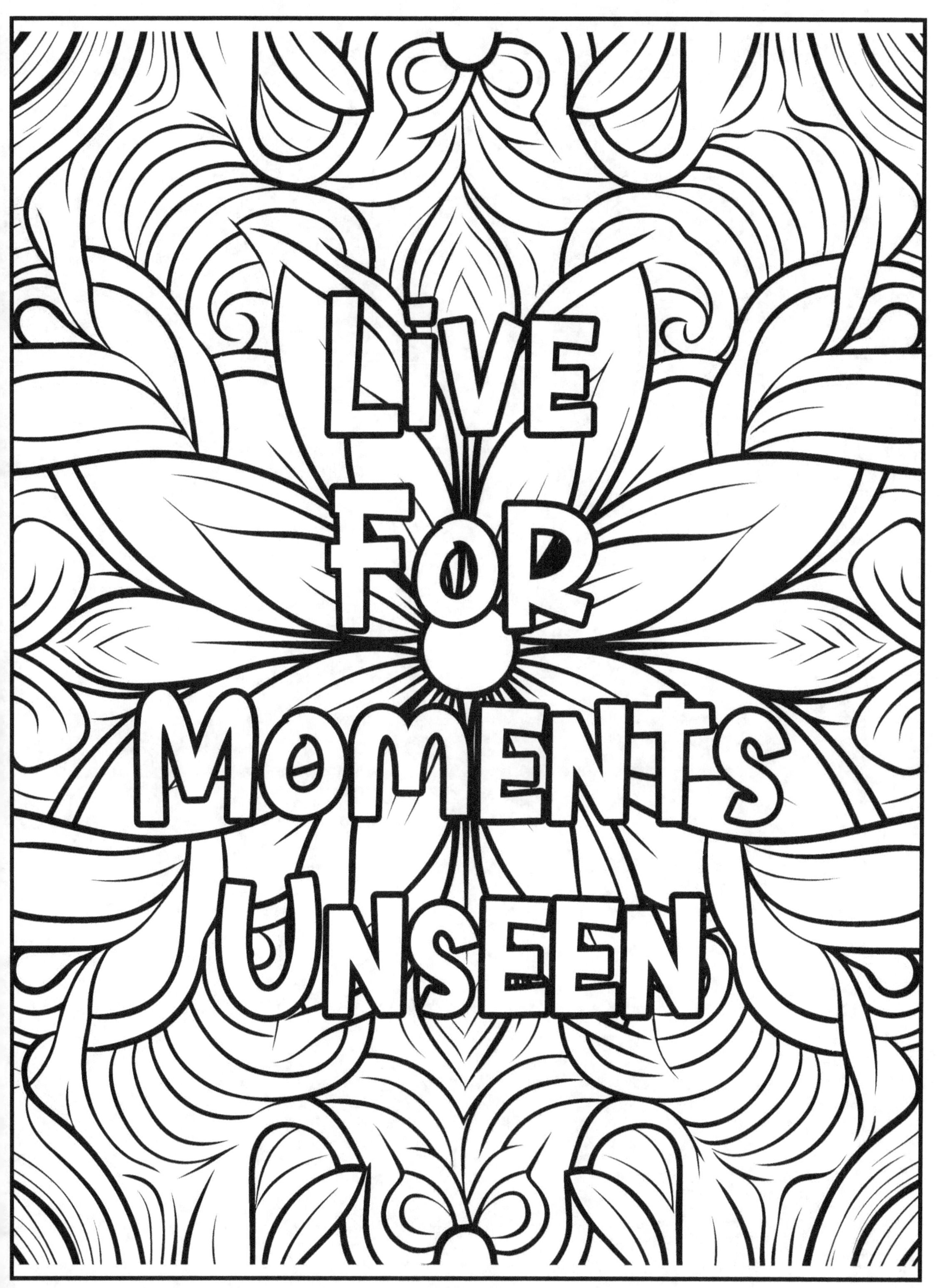

Live
For
Moments
Unseen

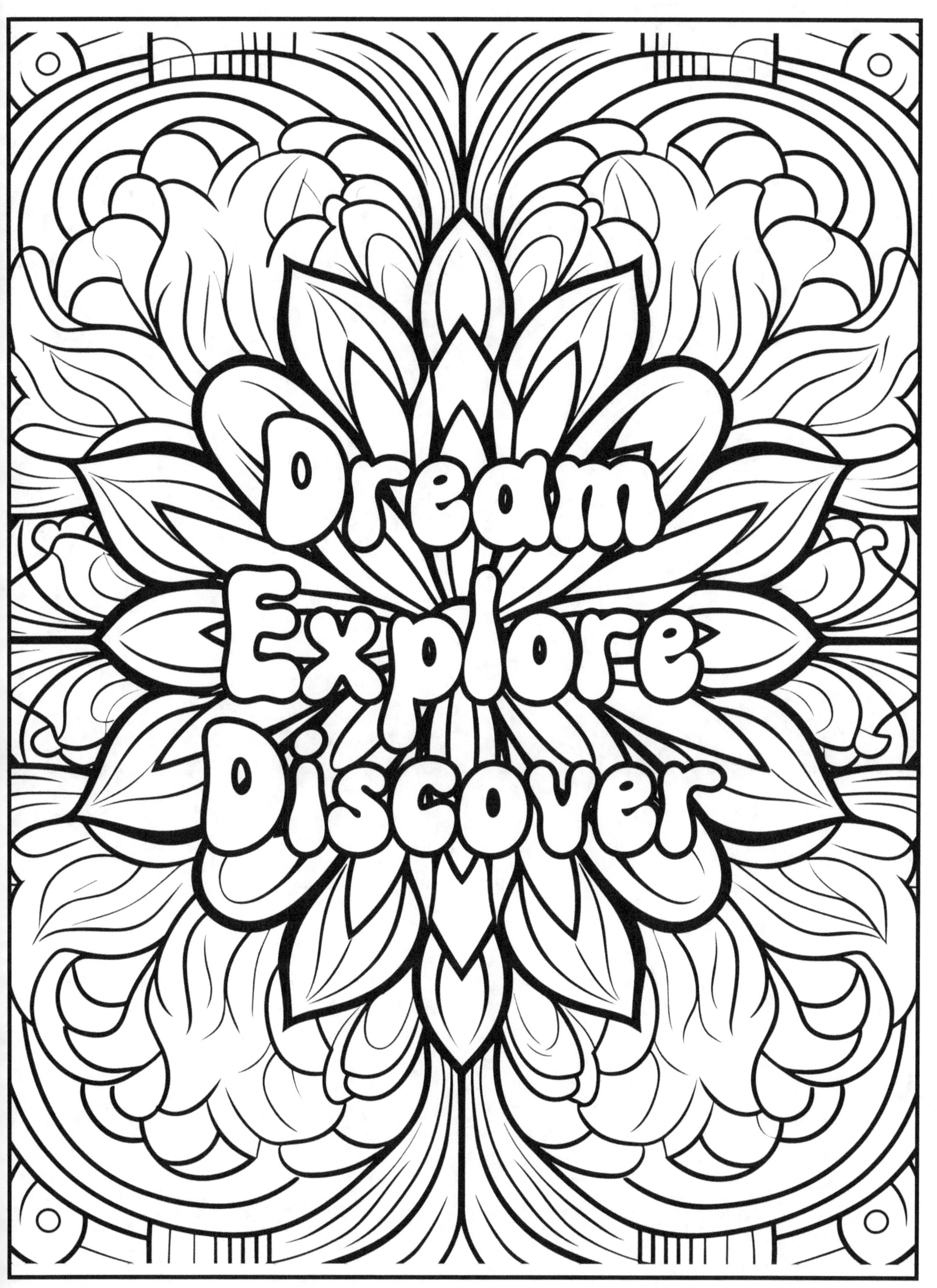

Dream
Explore
Discover

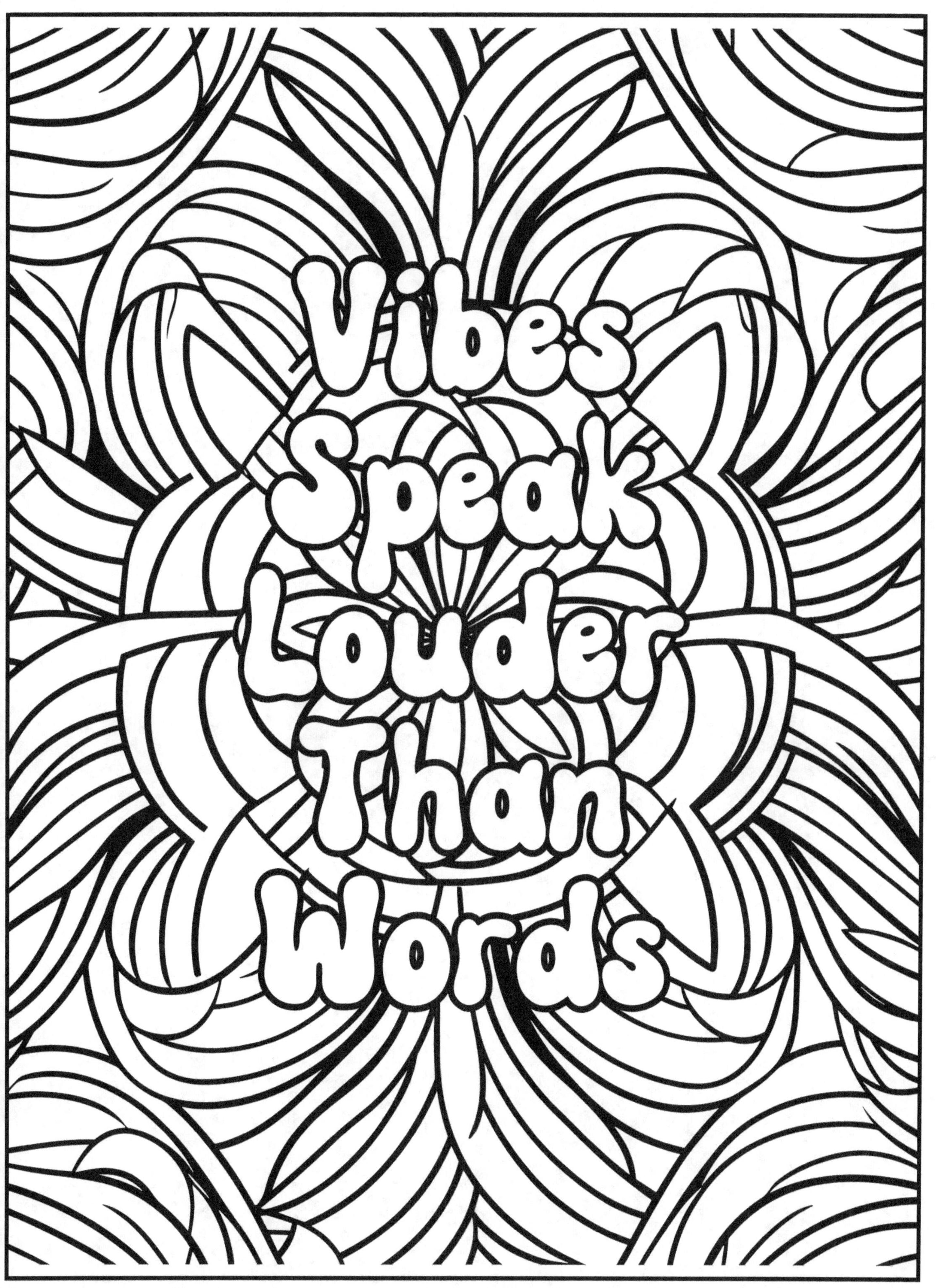

Vibes
Speak
Louder
Than
Words

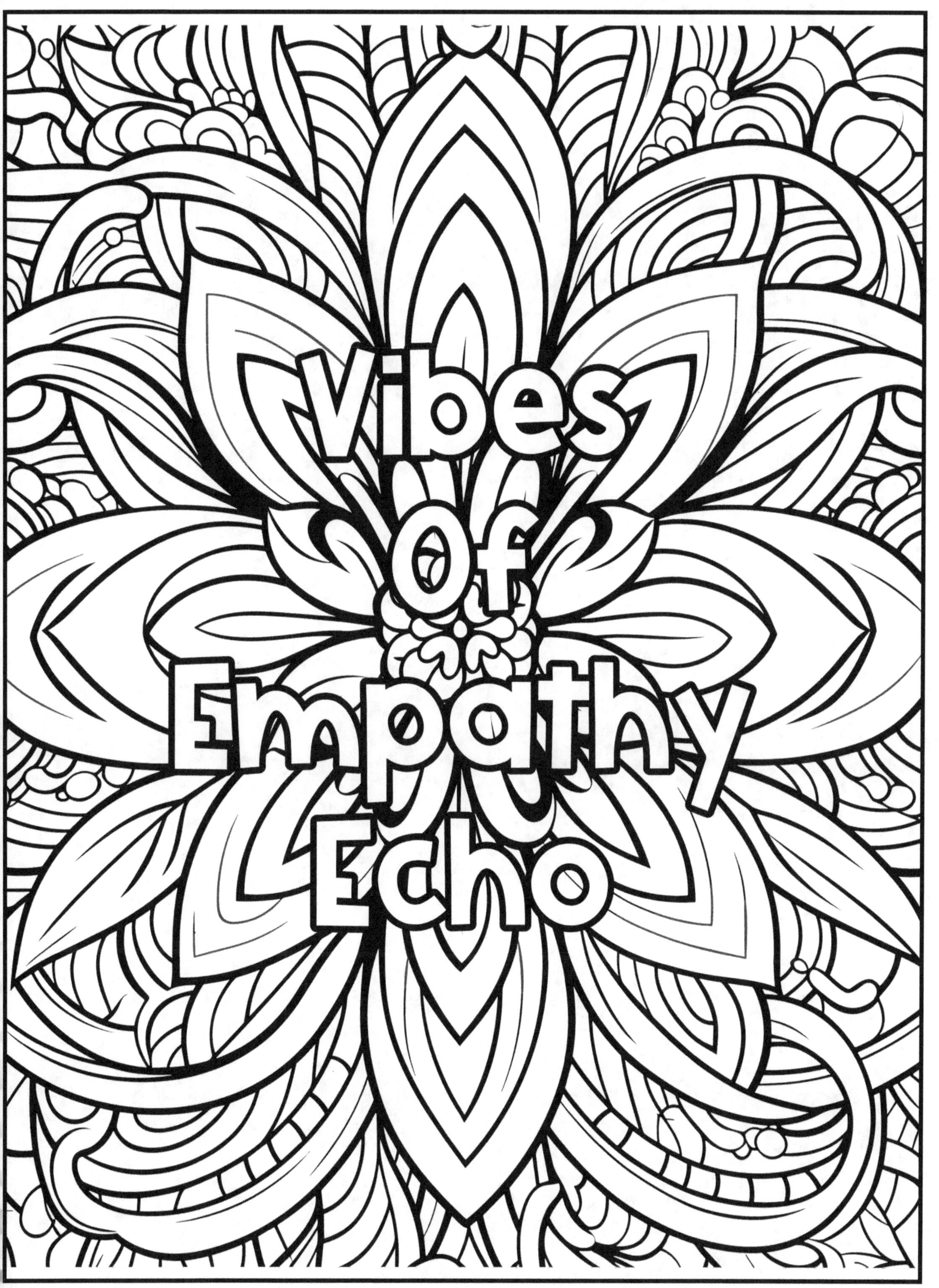

Vibes
Of
Empathy
Echo

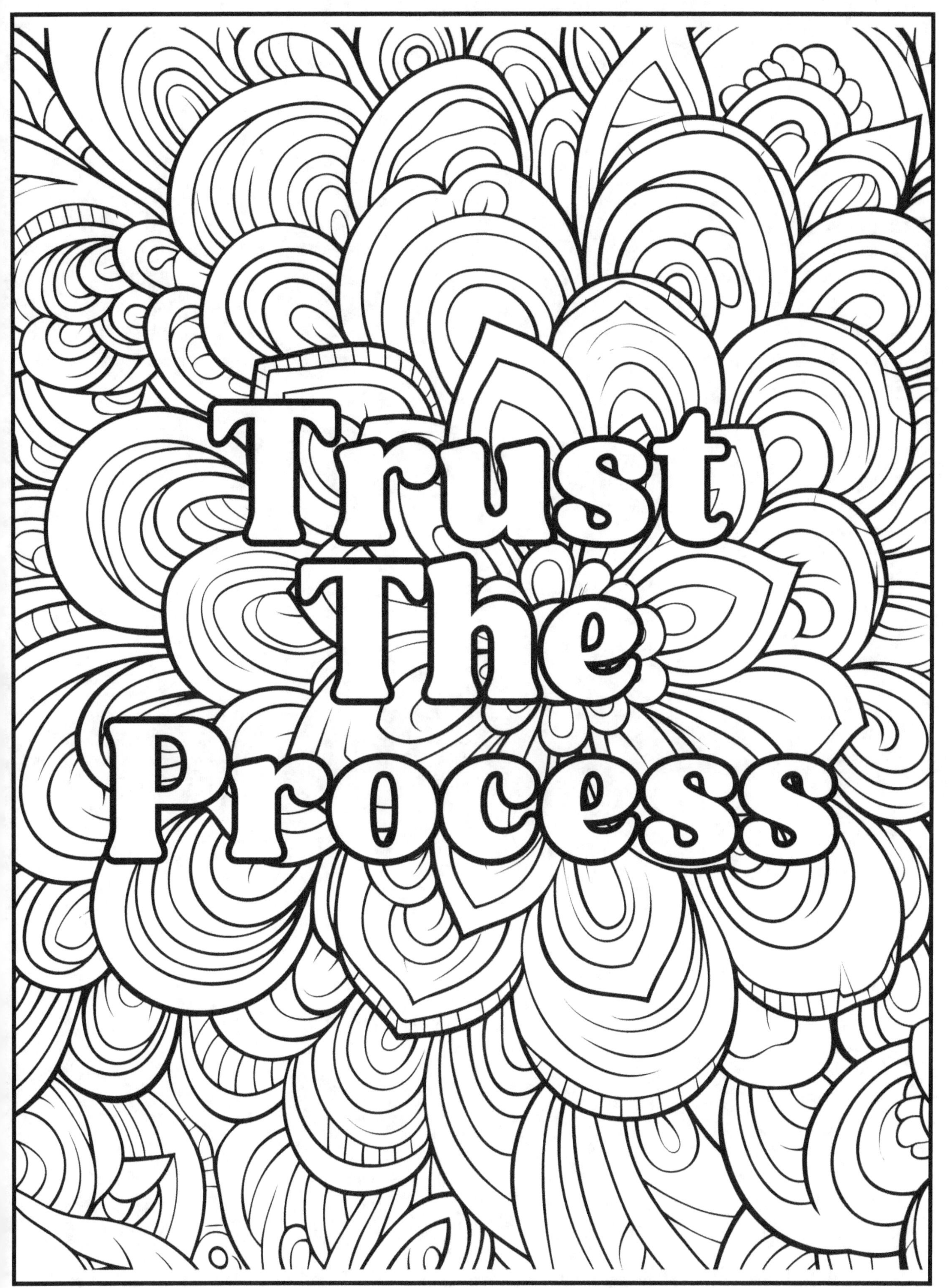

Trust
The
Process

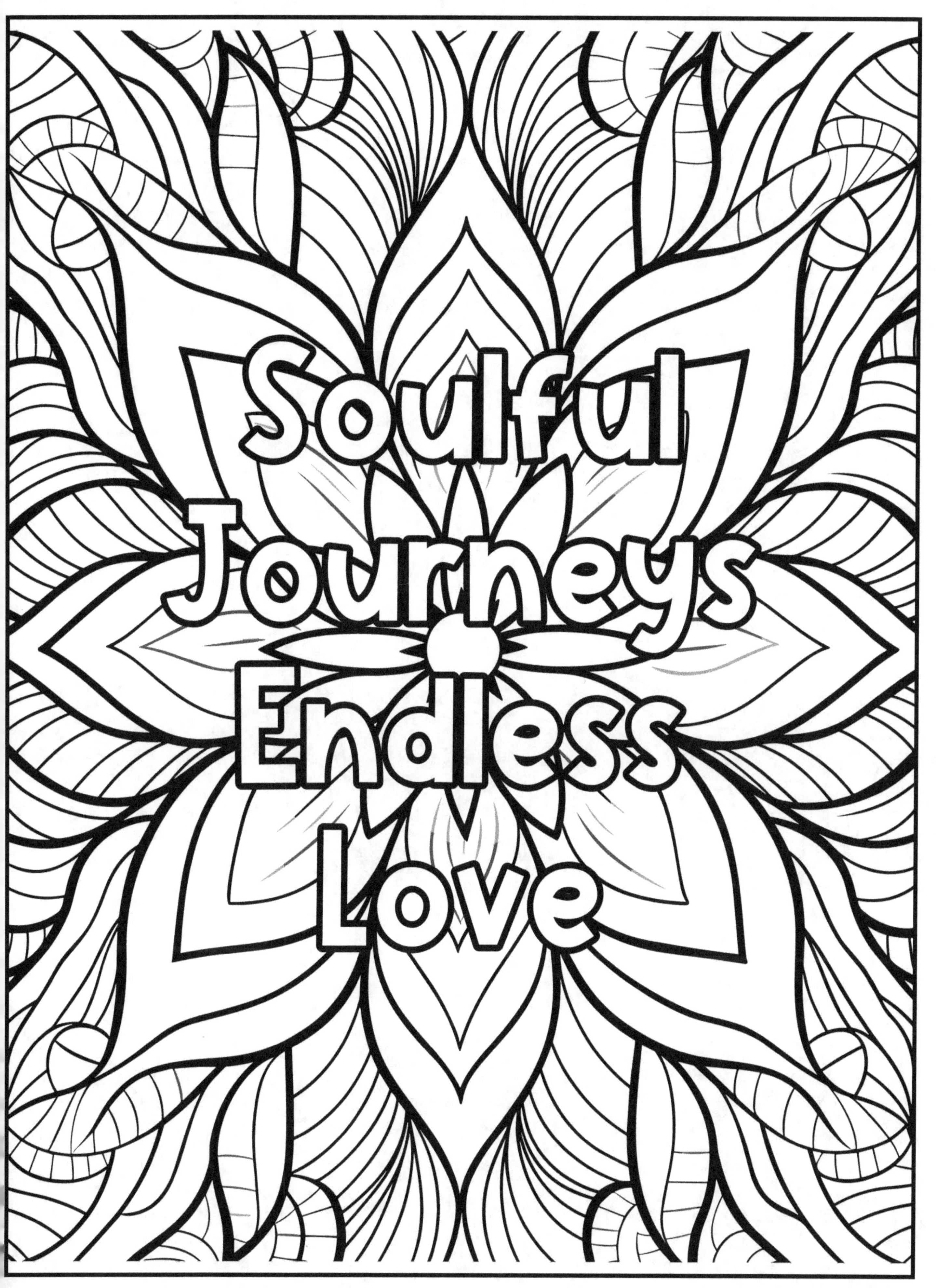
Soulful
Journeys
Endless
Love

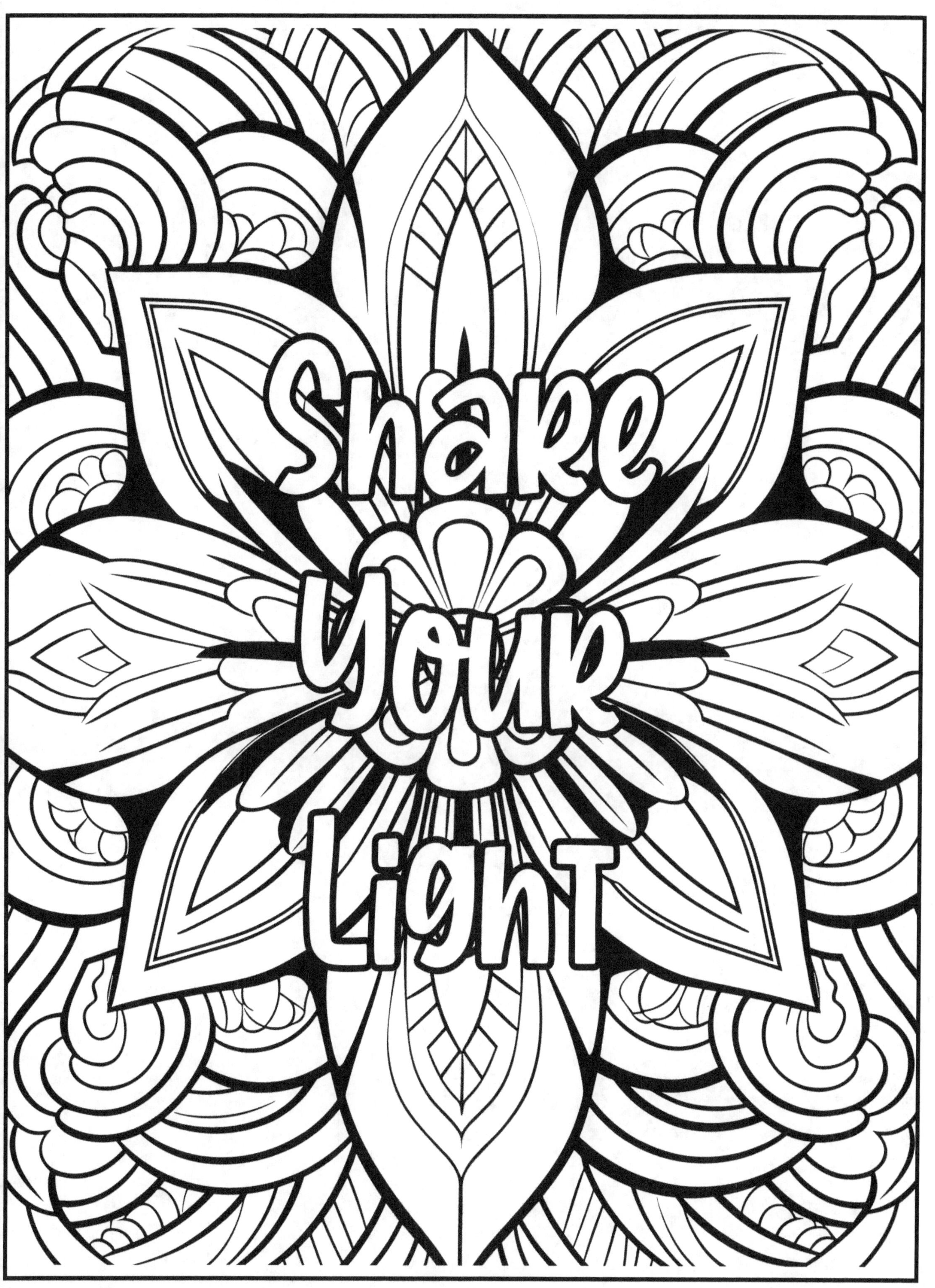
Shake
Your
Light

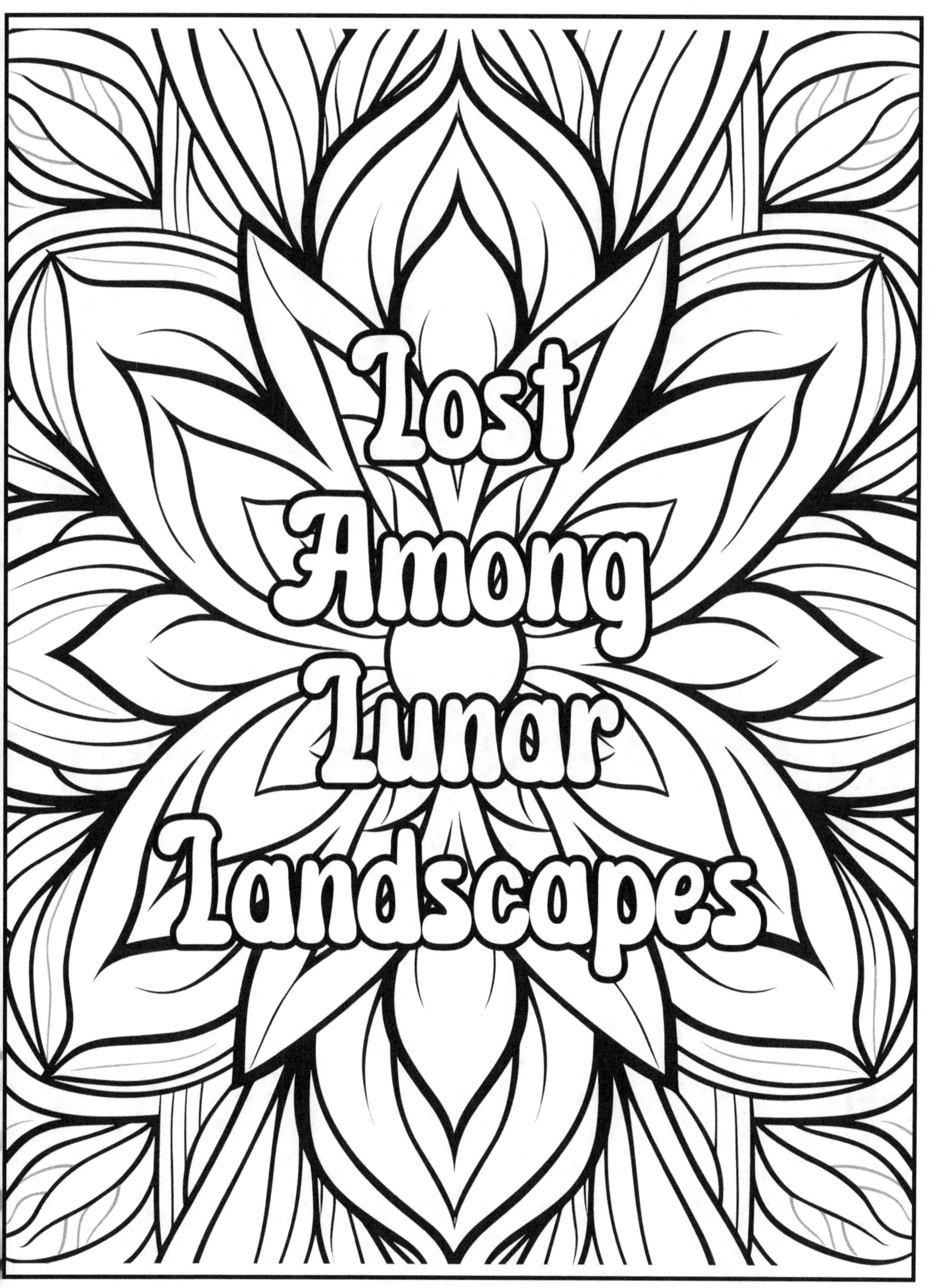

Lost
Among
Lunar
Landscapes

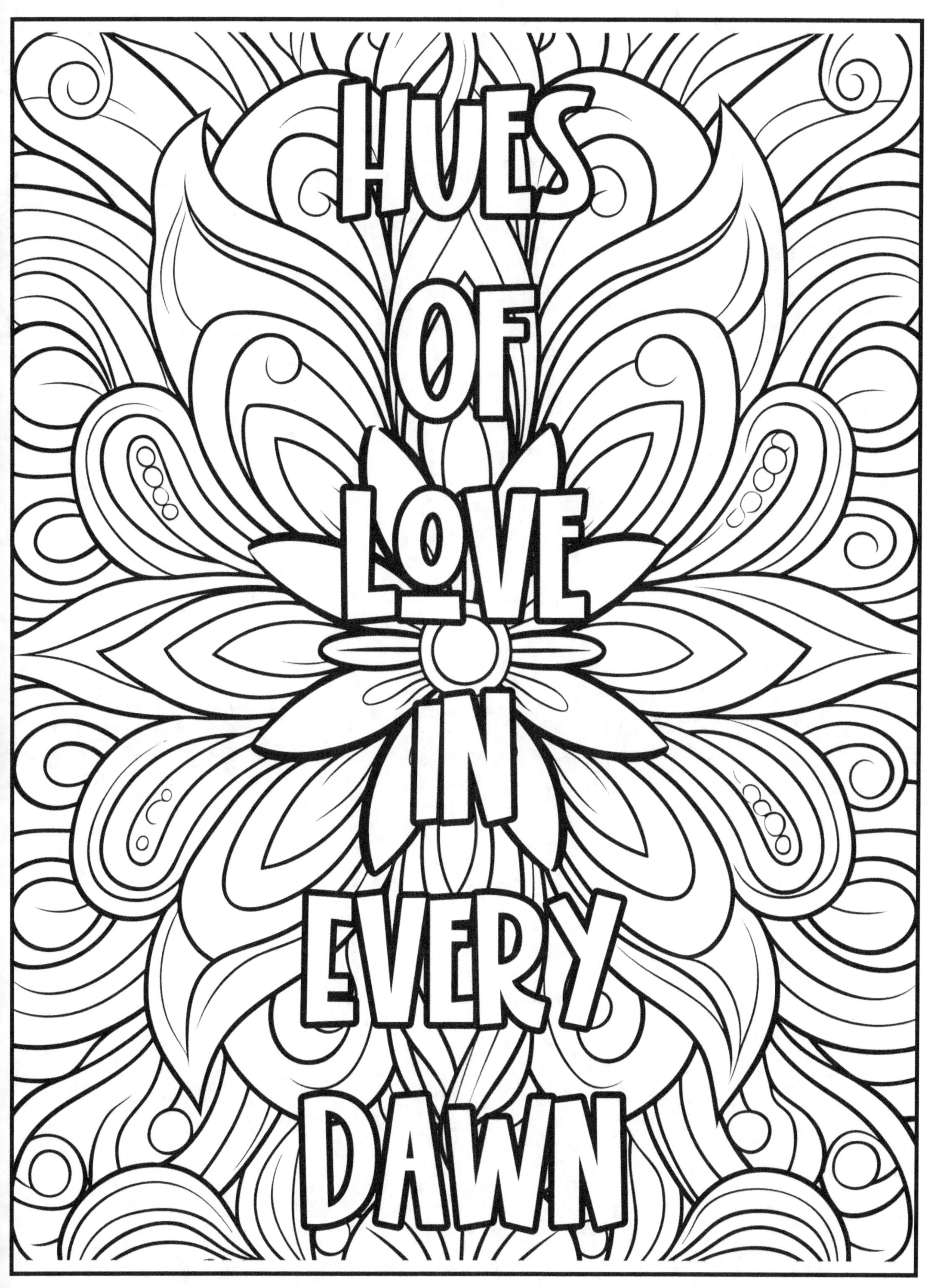

HUES
OF
LOVE
IN
EVERY
DAWN

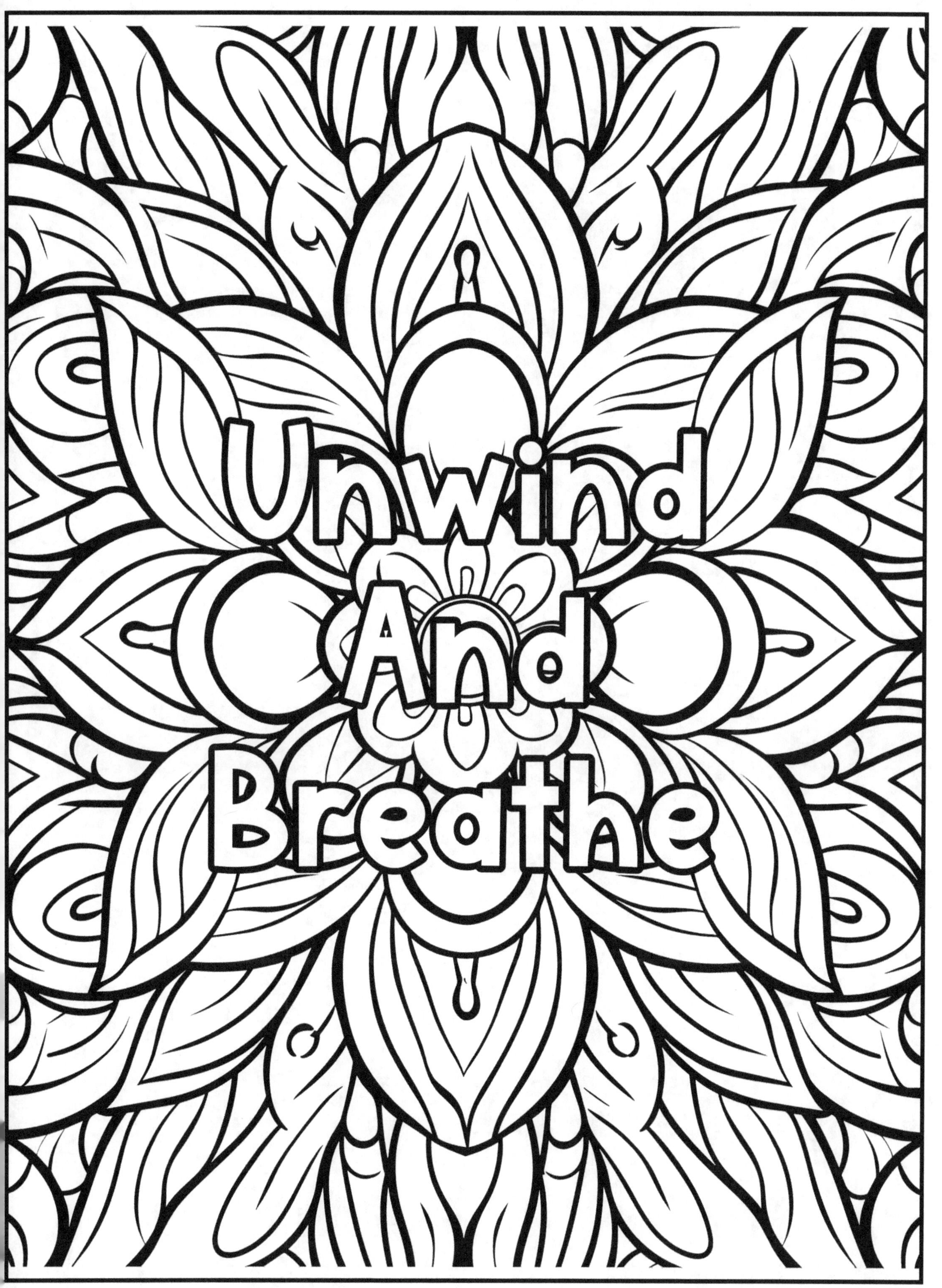

Unwind
And
Breathe

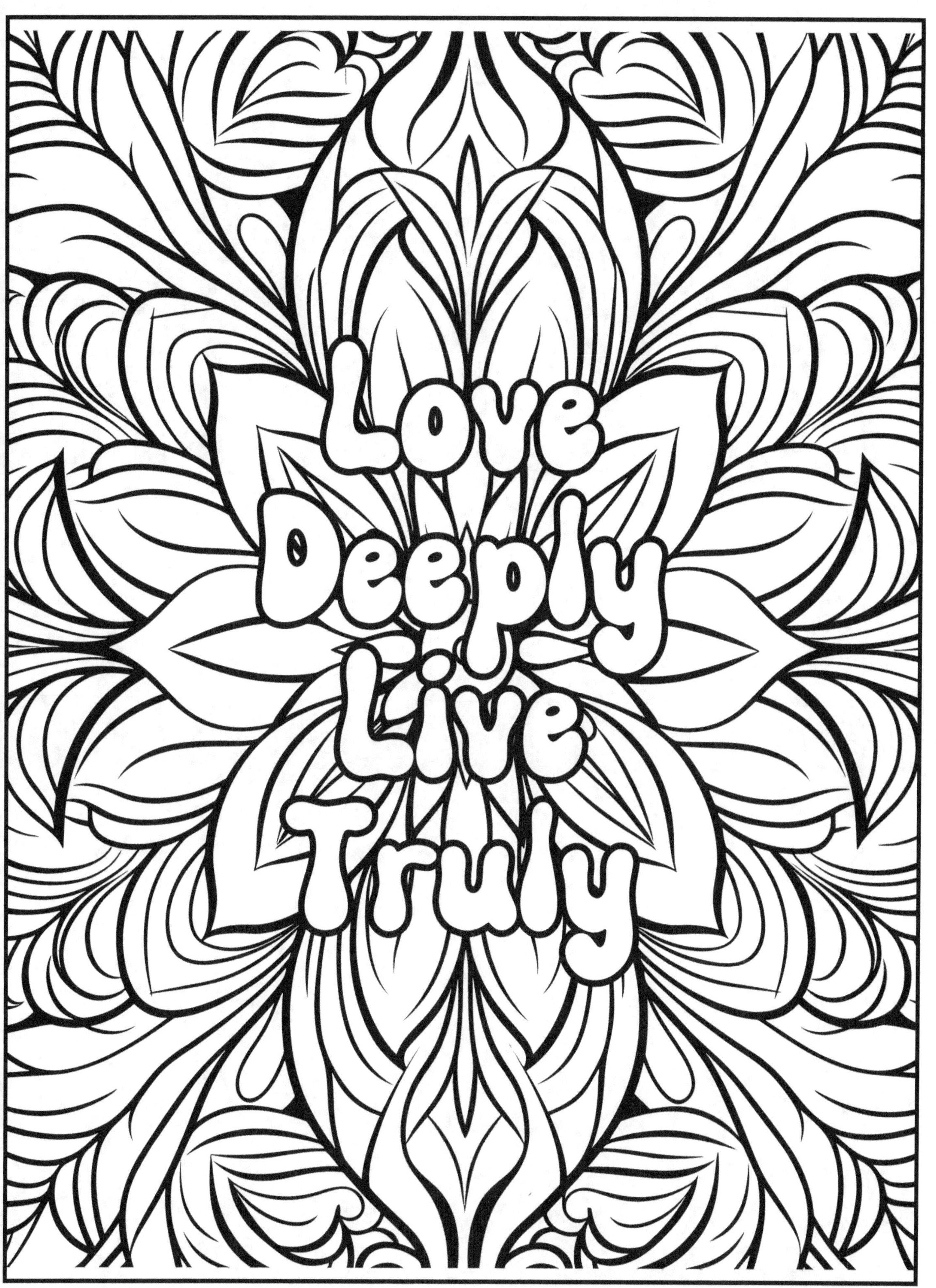

Love
Deeply
Live
Truly

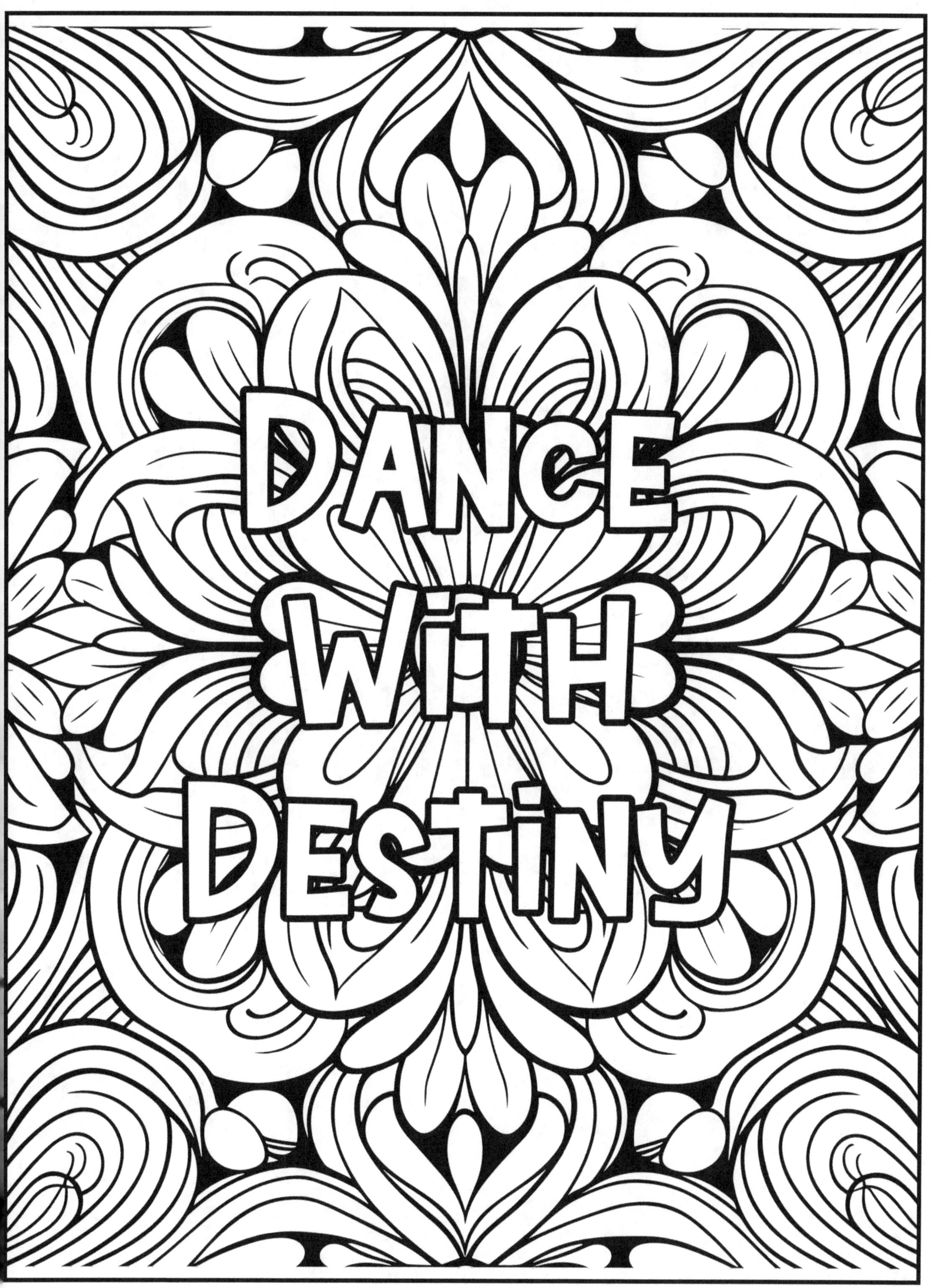

DANCE
WITH
DESTINY

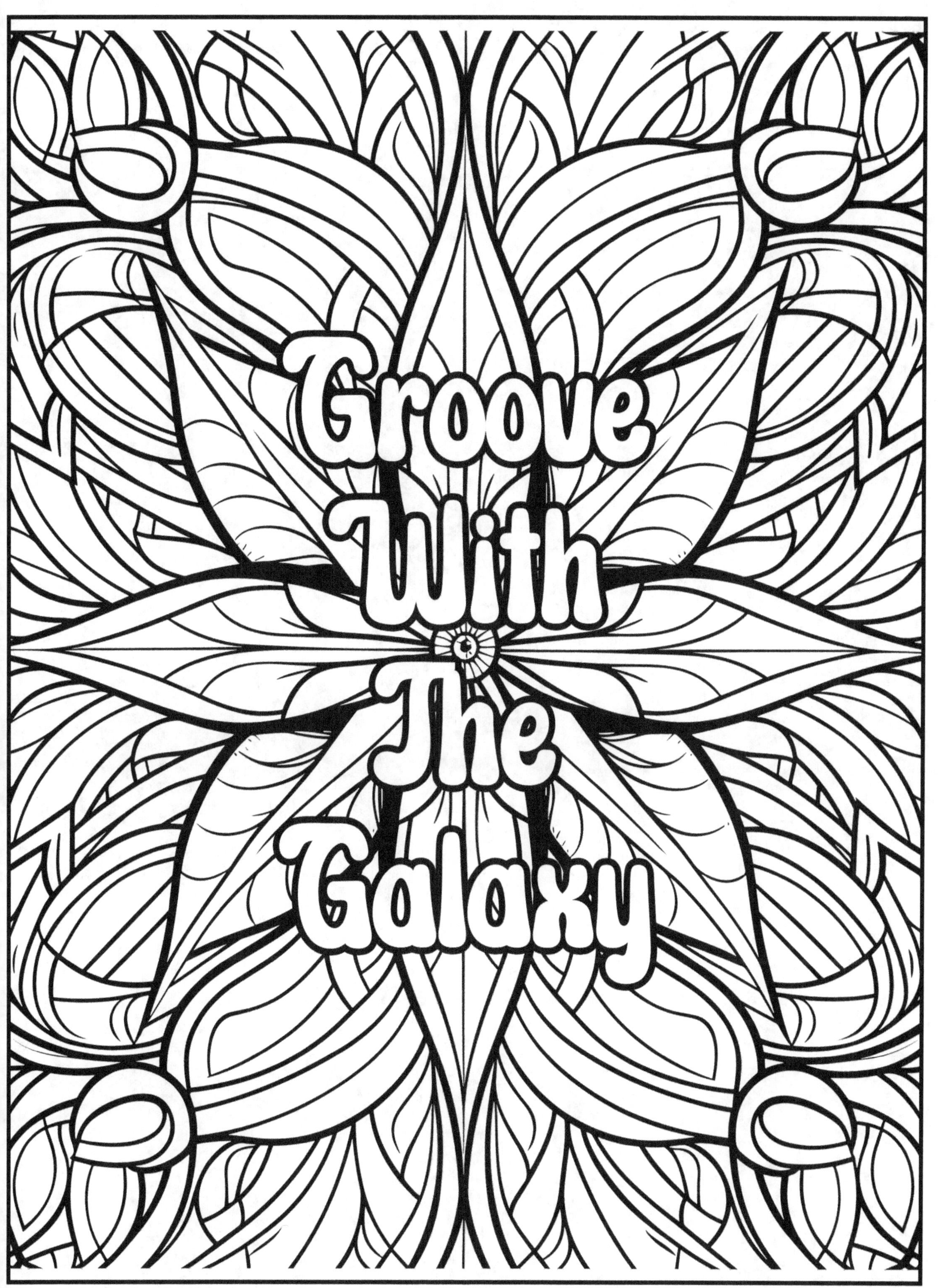

Groove
With
The
Galaxy

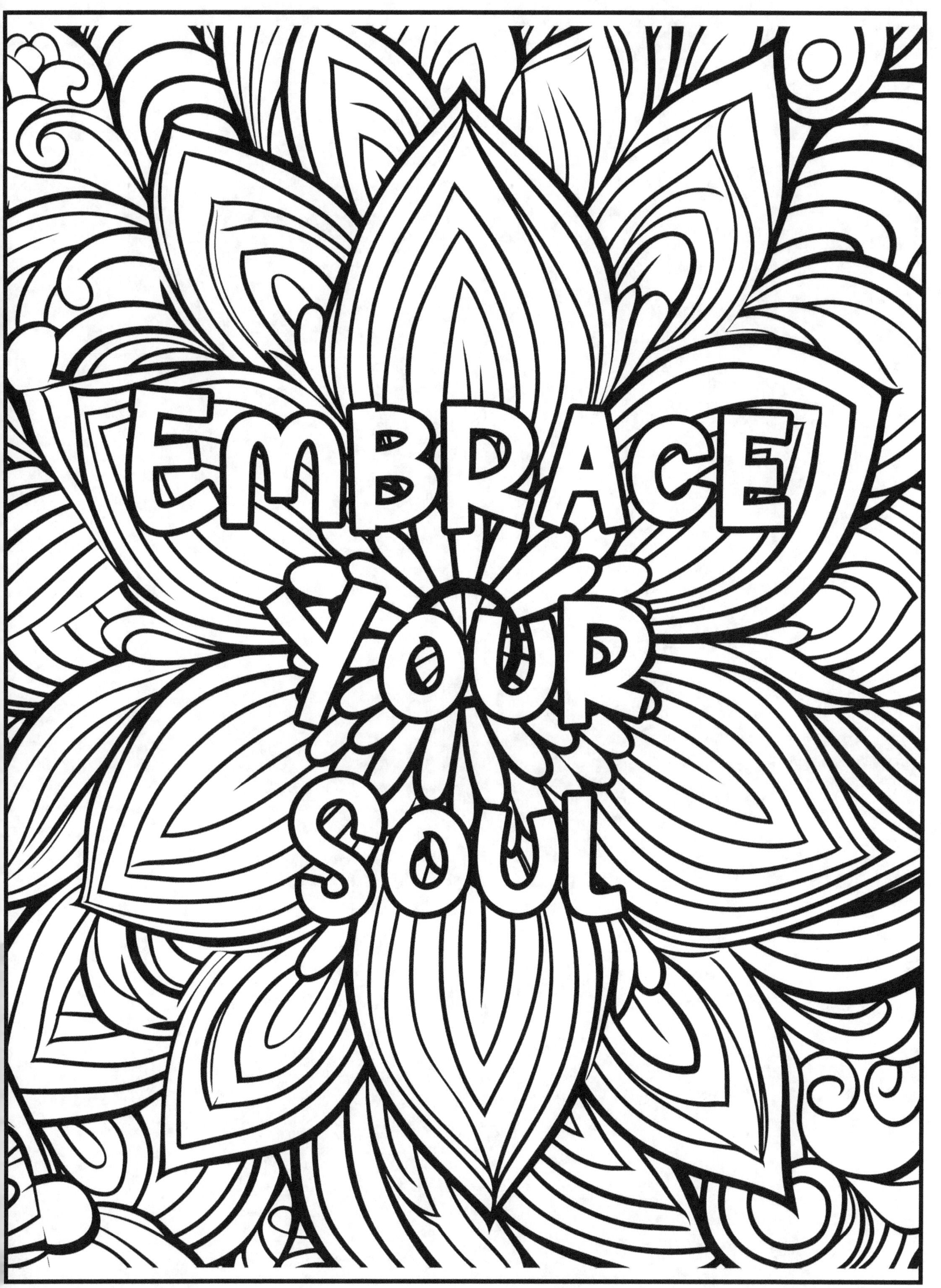

EMBRACE
YOUR
SOUL

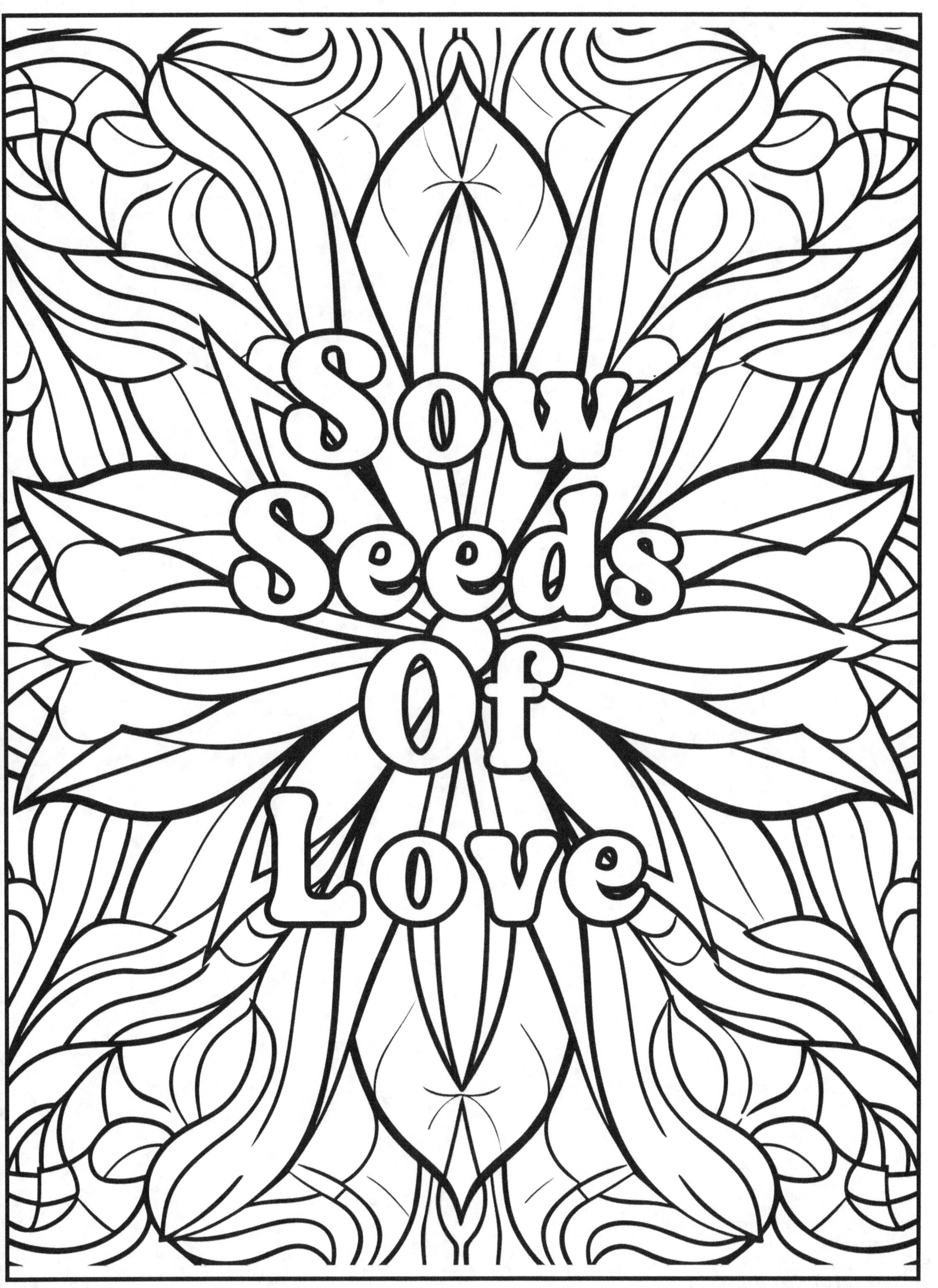

Sow
Seeds
Of
Love

www.ingramcontent.com/pod-product-compliance
Lightning Source LLC
Chambersburg PA
CBHW080939260726
48661CB00010B/3986